Genetics:
An Experimental Approach
Second Edition

Dr. Catherine E. Steding
Indiana State University
Department of Biology
The Rich and Robin Porter Cancer Research Center
The Center for Genomic Advocacy

Acknowledgements

For Gary, Lyla, and Kylie

All ventures big and small require support and assistance.
Significant assistance with the development of this manual was provided by my
department and colleagues both past and present.

Genetics Laboratory Manual

Table of Contents

Genetics Laboratory Manual

Introduction

This manual is designed to be a companion manual to a basic course in Genetics. It is important that you read the exercises carefully before attending the lab session each week. There are pre-laboratory questions mixed into each exercise that are critical to the successful completion of the exercises. The pre-lab questions are due at the start of the lab period. If you attempt to answer these questions during the lab, not only will you not get full credit for the assignment, you likely will not have time to complete the procedures.

Depending on time constraints and equipment availability, the laboratory exercises to be performed may change. Be sure to check with your instructor 1 week prior to the lab session to ensure you are preparing for the correct experiment. Additionally, the specific cells and other components are not always indicated in the exercises. This is intentional in order to enable variation based on available materials. Be sure to ask questions and pay attention to instructions in order to guarantee you have all the information you need to be successful.

As part of any laboratory, regardless of teaching or research, you will be expected to create and maintain a laboratory notebook. It is important in science that we keep track of all activities performed to enable rigorous review and reproducibility. With the goal of maintaining a consistent record of work completed in the lab, many of the pages in this text are designed to be removed and inserted into a binder or notebook.

This book is available through your university bookstore or on Amazon.com. If you purchased this book secondhand or through some other source, you are likely missing many pages critical to successful completion of the laboratory exercises. Verify that you have pre-laboratory questions and post-laboratory exercises/information with each laboratory before beginning the class. If you do not, then you will need to replace your manual and that may result in additional cost. As they say, "caveat emptor" so make sure you are exercising due diligence.

Laboratory Safety Policies and Procedures

Obtaining a complete understanding of Biology requires an experiential approach. There are some things that you simply must do in order to fully learn them. Successful training in biological experimental techniques requires proper training. Training is necessary to ensure both proper completion of experiments leading to useable data and, perhaps more importantly, safety. In this laboratory course, you will be expected to handle a variety of hazardous materials. This section of the manual is designed to review basic laboratory policies and safety procedures.

A laboratory in some ways is a regular classroom with the potential for explosive consequences. All of the regular classroom obligations of respect and consideration should be followed. Additionally, a laboratory, unlike a regular classroom, requires precautions to protect all personnel. Safety should always be a top priority. Occupational Health and Safety establishes guidelines for the proper handling and disposal of hazardous materials. Based on their recommendations, several rules and regulations exist. These are not mere suggestions. They are regulations designed for your safety. If you disregard them, you do so at your own risk.

In this course, you may utilize hazardous materials that represent either a chemical hazard or a biological one. Regardless of the specific hazard, the following guidelines should be followed:

General Safety Guidelines

1. **Follow all written and oral instructions.** Instructions are designed to assist you in the successful completion of your experiments as well as to ensure you protect yourself and others from harm.

2. **Do NOT wear clothing you like or want to keep "nice".** Working in a laboratory is "dirty" business. We handle chemicals, dyes, and stains; all of which are capable of ruining clothing. Even though lab coats are worn, they are hardly infallible and accidents do happen. Please always keep this in mind and plan accordingly.

3. **There is absolutely no eating or drinking in the lab. This includes chewing gum.**

4. **Wash your hands before leaving the laboratory.** The very last thing you should do in any lab is wash your hands. This is after cleaning up the lab and <u>before</u> you gather your personal items. Do NOT touch anything you don't wish to contaminate until after you have cleaned your hands. It is also important to wash your hands, or at least change your gloves, after handling Biohazardous materials and before handling non-Biohazardous materials.

5. **Do not apply make-up or insert contact lenses in the laboratory.** This has the potential to trap toxins against your eye and skin.

6. **Do not talk on or use your cell phones unless you are told it is safe.** Cell phones can pose a unique health hazard if contaminated by laboratory materials as they are difficult to clean. Never handle your phone while wearing gloves.

7. **Come to the laboratory fully prepared to perform the experiments.** Reading and preparing for experiments is critical to completing them in the time allotted and to maintaining safety.

8. **Know the laboratory space.** Be sure to identify where all of the personal safety equipment is located as well as the emergency exits. This equipment includes: the sink for hand washing, all eye washes, fire extinguisher, emergency shower, chemical spill kit, old timey wall phone, and first aid kit.

9. **Keep your work area as clean as possible throughout all experimental procedures.** All personal items should be stored away from the work surface. All spills should be cleaned immediately. This will prevent accidental contact with hazardous materials. Additionally, all tools should be returned to their proper places upon conclusion of the laboratory procedure.

10. **Always be aware of your surroundings.** If you need to walk around the room, especially when carrying hazardous items, it is YOUR responsibility to communicate with others in the lab. Additionally, you should avoid moving around unnecessarily. Be a "defensive" walker and always keep an eye out for others. This is crucial to avoid bumping into one another.

11. **If anything gets in your eyes, immediately seek assistance and head to an eyewash station.** These stations take two people to properly operate. Hold your eyes open and flush them for a minimum of 15 minutes. If you wear contact lenses, be aware that they inhibit proper rinsing of your eyes and can complicate chemical spills. If possible, wear glasses when chemical hazards are going to be present.

12. **When in doubt, talk with your instructor.** If you have any questions or concerns, discuss them with your instructor. The responsibility for your safety ultimately lies with YOU.

Personal Protective Equipment (PPE)

1. Gloves and laboratory coats should be worn throughout all experimental procedures. Laboratory coats should be removed and placed in plastic bags at the end of the session to avoid spreading contaminants outside the laboratory.

2. Eye protection such as goggles or face shields should be worn when hazards are present.

3. Masks should be worn when inhalation hazards are present. A chemical fume hood should be utilized for significant inhalation hazards. You will be advised as to which is appropriate or you may refer to the MSDA for each chemical.

4. Proper laboratory attire is required to participate in experimental procedures. Closed toe shoes are required in the event of chemical spills. Excessively loose clothing should be avoided. If you are not wearing appropriate clothing, you will be asked to leave and it will be counted as an unexcused absence.

Handling Laboratory Equipment

1. **If you don't know what it is for or how to use it properly, do NOT touch it.** Some equipment can be damaged when touched with ungloved hands or may simply be very sensitive to manipulation. Unless you have been trained or instructed on how to use or handle something, it is best to leave it alone.

2. **Laboratory equipment is often expensive.** If your negligence or direct intent results in damage to a piece of equipment, you may be expected to replace the item. Intentional damaging of laboratory equipment will be considered a violation of the Code of Student Conduct.

3. **Microscopes require particular care to avoid damage.** Microscopes should be carried upright with one hand under the base and one hand on the arm. Oil immersion should only be used when instructed that it is necessary. Use of oil on the wrong optics can cause significant damage. All lenses and optics should be cleaned after use with appropriate, microscope-approved materials free of particulates.

4. **Examine all equipment before use.** Careful inspection of equipment PRIOR to use can ensure that unsafe equipment is not used and that you will not be held responsible for causing damage you did not cause. Report any damaged or malfunctioning equipment to your instructor.

Clean-up Procedures

1. In the event of chemical spills, follow the specific instructions for each chemical to determine the proper procedure for cleaning and disposing of the chemical (see MSDS). Your instructor will have this information and can assist you. Chemical spill kits are located in every lab. It is YOUR responsibility to notify your instructor whenever spills occur.

2. If you spill acids or other corrosive or hazardous chemicals on your person, flush the site with copious amounts of water. A minimum of 15 minutes is required to adequately flush a chemical from skin or your eyes. If the spill is

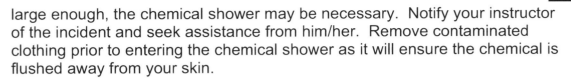

large enough, the chemical shower may be necessary. Notify your instructor of the incident and seek assistance from him/her. Remove contaminated clothing prior to entering the chemical shower as it will ensure the chemical is flushed away from your skin.

3. The laboratory should be cleaned at the end of each session. You will not be permitted to leave until the lab is returned to the physical condition in which you found it. This includes sanitizing benches with the 10% bleach solution or 70% ethanol as required by the experimental conditions. Experiment-specific clean-up procedures will be provided during the session.

4. Dispose of all chemical waste properly. Most of the liquid materials utilized in this lab can be disposed of down the drain and flushed with water. Each chemical should be disposed of <u>individually</u> under running water to avoid mixing. Solid chemical waste should be placed in the appropriate disposal containers. Your instructor will provide instructions on the proper disposal of such chemicals.

5. Dispose of all plastic and paper waste properly. You will be advised as to whether the waste is Biohazardous or capable of being disposed of in the traditional trash.

6. Some plastics can be reused. Follow instructions regarding the proper handling and cleaning of the reusable items.

7. Biohazardous waste must be disposed of in the proper biohazard containers.

8. Broken glass and sharps must be disposed of in puncture proof containers. Glass disposal boxes are utilized for glass while red plastic containers are utilized for sharps. Both types of these containers can be found near the trash and Biohazardous waste containers. Do NOT pick up broken or sharp items directly with your hands. Tongs and other safety items are available for proper clean-up and disposal to minimize risk of injury.

The first line of defense for all laboratory work is the personal protective equipment:

Failure to wear this most basic equipment is asking for unnecessary injury. Specific chemical and biological hazards may require additional equipment or safety precautions. You MUST pay careful attention to your instructor to ensure you are utilizing best practices in the laboratory environment. When in doubt, ask questions and be your own advocate for your own safety!

Safety Training Documentation Assignment 1: What's wrong with this picture?

One or more things may be inappropriate or unsafe in the following pictures. Please indicate what errors in safety are being represented by each picture in the space provided.

Laboratory Policies and Procedures/Safety Agreement

Course Title: _____

Term: _____

Section Day/Time: _____

I have carefully read and understand all polices, rules, and regulations associated with participating in the laboratory exercises accompanying this course. I agree to follow all regulations and understand that my safety is ultimately my responsibility.

Specifically,
1. I agree to come to class prepared
2. I agree to pay careful attention to all instructions
3. I agree to only perform the work outlined by the course under the supervision of the instructor
4. I agree to wear the proper safety equipment
5. I agree to conduct myself in a professional manner
6. I agree to make safety a priority
7. I agree to ask questions and seek guidance when confused or uncertain

Print Name: _____

Signature: _____

Date: _____

Exercise 1
Introduction to Pipetting

Objectives

1. Begin utilizing pipetmen in experiments
2. Learn to test the accuracy of pipetmen
3. Learn the limitations for accuracy of pipetmen
4. Learn the concept of pipetable volume
5. Re-enforce accuracy in pipetting

Introduction

Genetics, like all fields that involve an understanding of Molecular Biology, requires us to grapple with very small volumes of liquids. Through this exercise you will refine the most basic of skills necessary to be successful utilizing molecular techniques. This exercise will also reinforce the importance of accurate pipetting in order to improve the chance for success throughout all future exercises in this course.

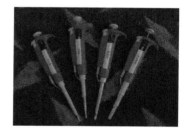

Of all the basic tools utilized in molecular research, pipetmen are among the most important. Pipetmen enable us to perform molecular experiments by allowing us to transfer extremely small volumes of liquids. The pipetmen you will most likely encounter in the laboratory include a P2, P10, P20, P200, and P1000. The size of the pipetman you have in hand can be determined in two ways.

The top of the dial provides information on some pipetmen. From left to right the image below shows the P1000, P200, P20, and P10. They can even be color-coded.

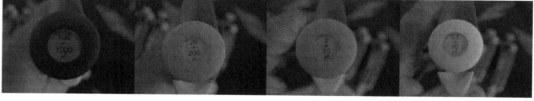

The tip of the pipetmen also gives away information about which size you have in hand. From left to right the image to the left shows the P1000, P200, P20, and P10.

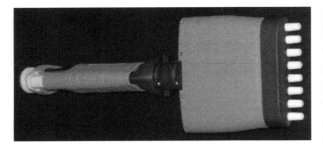

For large scale experiments, it can be ideal for reproducibility to use a pipet with more than one channel, the multichannel pipette. These enable rapid and consistent pipetting into 96 well plates. A multichannel pipetman typically accommodates 8 or 12 tips simultaneously.

Although each pipetman seems to be capable of pulling up the full range of volumes based on the dials, there is a limit of *accuracy* to all pipetmen; a maximum and minimum volume that the pipetman will accurately pipet.

A P2 can accurately pipet 0.5 μl to 2 μl.
A P10 can accurately pipet 0.5 μl to 10 μl.
A P20 can accurately pipet 2 μl to 20 μl.
A P200 can accurately pipet 20 μl to 200 μl.
A P1000 can accurately pipet 200 μl to 1000 μl.

Each pipetman has 3 numbers to indicate how much you are pipetting. Only the P200 indicates the literal volume by number. What this means is that a P20 being used to pipet 20 μl reads 2, 0, 0, while, a P200 shows 0, 2, 0 (see Figure 1).

0	A P1000 ready	2	A P200 ready to	0	A P200 ready to	2	A P20 ready to
2	to pipet 200 μl	0	pipet 200 μl	2	pipet 20 μl	0	pipet 20 μl
0	looks like 020	0	looks like 200	0	looks like 020	0	looks like 200

Figure 1. Pipetmen Pipetting Indicator Windows.

Whenever you pipet, it is best to utilize the smallest pipetman you can to accurately pipet the required volume. This is particularly important in situations where you want to avoid excessive mixing. Repeated attempts to pipet too much or too little liquid can break the pipetmen. This is especially true if you pipet liquid up into the internal components of a pipetman. Should you accidently pull liquid into a pipetman, it must be cleaned immediately to avoid corrosion or permanent damage. Each pipetman can be broken down for cleaning and repairs. Do not attempt to breakdown or clean pipetmen without instruction. It is important to maintain pipetmen to ensure long-term viability and accuracy.

Typically, pipetmen are calibrated once a year as needed; however, before using pipetmen in important experiments, you must ensure that they are working properly and are accurate. There are quick checks that can be performed to demonstrate the accuracy of the pipetmen in between calibrations. This lab is designed to perform those quick checks and reinforce proper pipetting techniques.

Part A
Testing Pipetman Accuracy

Noteworthy Information:

Albert Einstein once said, "Strive not to be a success, but rather to be of value".

In Science, the outcome is often far less important than the journey. Having to troubleshoot experiments enables us to fully understand not just "what" we are doing but also "how" we are doing it. We learn far more about the "how" from our mistakes than we do from perfect success.

1 milliliter of pure water weighs 1 gram
1000 µl equals 1 milliliter

Pre-Laboratory Questions

1. Based on the information provided, how much should each of the following volumes weigh in both *grams* and *milligrams*:

0.5 µl _____   1 µl _____   2 µl _____

10 µl _____   20 µl _____   100 µl _____

200 µl _____   500 µl _____   1000µl _____

2. If it is only acceptable to utilize a pipet that distributes volumes within a 5% margin of error, what is the maximum and minimum weight in *milligrams* for each of the volumes listed below for the pipetman to still be considered accurate:

0.5 µl _____ & _____   1 µl _____ & _____

2 µl _____ & _____   10 µl _____ & _____

20 µl _____ & _____   100 µl _____ & _____

200 µl _____ & _____   500 µl _____ & _____

1000µl _____ & _____

Procedure: Testing the quality and accuracy of your equipment

This procedure may not be completed as part of your laboratory exercise depending on equipment availability and time allotted. You should note that if you do NOT evaluate the quality and accuracy of your equipment, you cannot determine whether errors observed at the end of the experiment were the result of user error or equipment error.

1. Place a weigh boat onto the balance provided and zero the balance

2. Pipet reverse osmosis purified water (ROH_2O) into the weigh boat one at a time in the volumes listed below with the indicated pipetman

3. Repeat each volume 3 times; Be sure to dry the weigh boat completely in between each measurement

Results

NOTE: You may not have all of the following pipetment. Make changes as necessary and utilize the space provided on the next page to add any additional information or results.

P10
Pipet 1 µl: Weight 1: _____   Weight 2: _____   Weight 3: _____
Pipet 5 µl: Weight 1: _____   Weight 2: _____   Weight 3: _____
Pipet 10 µl: Weight 1: _____   Weight 2: _____   Weight 3: _____

P20
Pipet 2 µl: Weight 1: _____   Weight 2: _____   Weight 3: _____
Pipet 10 µl: Weight 1: _____   Weight 2: _____   Weight 3: _____
Pipet 20 µl: Weight 1: _____   Weight 2: _____   Weight 3: _____

P200
Pipet 20 µl: Weight 1: _____   Weight 2: _____   Weight 3: _____
Pipet 100 µl: Weight 1: _____   Weight 2: _____   Weight 3: _____
Pipet 200 µl: Weight 1: _____   Weight 2: _____   Weight 3: _____

P1000
Pipet 200 µl: Weight 1: _____   Weight 2: _____   Weight 3: _____
Pipet 500 µl: Weight 1: _____   Weight 2: _____   Weight 3: _____
Pipet 1000µl: Weight 1: _____   Weight 2: _____   Weight 3: _____

Based on the information provided and the data you obtained, are your pipetmen accurate? Explain your results. If you did NOT complete this exercise as part of the class, inspect the pipetmen and write your comments here.

_____
_____
_____
_____
_____
_____
_____
_____

Use the space below to make additional observations or record additional results. Be sure to note any issues or errors as you pipet. This can include any air bubbles or difficulties you have using the equipment. This space should be viewed as a place for recording your actions and thoughts.

Part B
Accurate Pipetting

Noteworthy Information:

Ralph Waldo Emerson wrote, "A foolish consistency is the hobgoblin of little minds, adored by little statesmen and philosophers and divines. With consistency a great soul has simply nothing to do."

In science, consistency is the gold standard. We strive to have accurate repeatable results that anyone following a protocol can achieve. This is how we establish facts from our observations to support or refute a hypothesis. In order for any hypothesis to reach the level of theory or law, it must withstand rigorous testing. This testing relies on consistent, reproducible, and accurate results. Using accurate pipetmen is only the first step to achieving accurate results. You must be able to use the pipetmen accurately and with consistency.

Pre-laboratory Questions:

There are no assigned pre-laboratory questions for this portion of the exercise. It is a very good idea to review Excel as the post-laboratory assignment will rely heavily on it. The following questions are designed to assist you in your review of the Excel program.

1. How do I determine the average of a set of data points/wells?
2. How do I determine the standard deviation of a set of data points/wells?
3. How do I select the appropriate graph type and insert a chart?
4. How do I add elements to a chart including error bars and trendlines?

Procedure: Pipetting Exercise

This exercise is designed to either introduce you to the concepts of pipetting or to reinforce pipetting techniques through practice. There is some repetition in this so be sure you are regularly checking the pipetmen and are pipetting with consistency.

In this exercise, you will use 2 different concentrations of a common dye, Methylene Blue. Methylene Blue is a dye that can be used for a variety of purposes with a well-established application in evaluating cellular proliferation (1). It is known to show correlative changes in absorbance with concentration and volume. Additionally, we are using it here because it has been shown to absorb light and produce accurate results at a range of wavelengths (610 nm to 650 nm) giving us the potential to have flexibility in case of limitations in equipment. By measuring the changes in absorbance of light using a standard plate reader, you will be able to assess how both your consistency and your accuracy in pipetting.

You may begin by adding either the water OR the dye depending on your equipment availability; however, you should carefully track your volumes to ensure proper dilution of the dye.

1. Add 5% Methylene Blue to each of the wells for the P20 and P1000 as indicated in Figure 2.

2. Add 1% Methylene Blue to each of the wells for the P200 as indicated in Figure 2.

3. Add Water to each of the wells of a 96 well plate as indicated in Figure 3. You should use the appropriate pipetman to complete this plate. This may be based on which one you have available to you. Please be sure to NOTE which one you used as it may have consequences on the outcome.

4. Read the absorbance at 630nm via a plate reader.

P20			P200			P200			P1000		
20	20	20	200	200	200	100	100	100	250	250	250
20	20	20	200	200	200	100	100	100	250	250	250
15	15	15	175	175	175	75	75	75	200	200	200
15	15	15	175	175	175	75	75	75	200	200	200
10	10	10	150	150	150	50	50	50	100	100	100
10	10	10	150	150	150	50	50	50	100	100	100
5	5	5	125	125	125	20	20	20	0	0	0
5	5	5	125	125	125	20	20	20	0	0	0

Figure 2. Methylene Blue Volumes. Using the pipetmen indicated at the top of the columns add the corresponding amount of methylene blue dye in *microliters* to the well.

P200			P200			P200			P200		
180	180	180	0	0	0	100	100	100	0	0	0
180	180	180	0	0	0	100	100	100	0	0	0
185	185	185	25	25	25	125	125	125	0	0	0
185	185	185	25	25	25	125	125	125	0	0	0
190	190	190	50	50	50	150	150	150	100	100	100
190	190	190	50	50	50	150	150	150	100	100	100
195	195	195	75	75	75	180	180	180	0	0	0
195	195	195	75	75	75	180	180	180	0	0	0

Figure 3. MilliQ Water Volumes. Using the pipetmen indicated at the top of the columns add the corresponding amount of water in *microliters* to the well.

All information obtained by the plate reader can be exported to Excel for analysis. You will need a flash drive to obtain your results.

Post-Laboratory Assignment

This assignment is designed to reinforce lessons in Excel, data analysis, and proper presentation of data.

Using Figure 1 as your guide, determine the average absorbance and the standard deviation for the 6 wells that correspond to each unique volume added per pipetman. These calculations can be performed easily using Excel.   Print the Excel spreadsheet with the average absorbance and standard deviation for each group of 6 wells.

Create a graph for each pipetman by graphing absorbance verses volume of methylene blue added. In the end, you should have 3 individual graphs. Add custom error bars using the standard deviation as the error. You are looking at the differences in absorbance across multiple volumes. This means you are interested in TRENDS and will need to include a trendline of your graphs as well as to define the slope and R value. Show the equation and R value on the graph.

Summarize your results in a word document that includes both a RESULTS section and a DISCUSSION section as outlined in the Appendix II of this manual.
.
The following questions should be used as a guide for content in these two sections:
1. Which type of graph is most appropriate? Which type of graph lets you make conclusions about changes over time or concentration? (NOTE: This question will be answered by your choice of graph).
2. What does your standard deviation tell you?
3. Is your standard deviation big or small?
4. What does the R value tell you about your accuracy?
5. Are the lines in the graphs relatively straight?
6. Based on your findings, how accurately did you pipet?

You will be expected to either print the report or submit it electronically prior to the start of your next laboratory session.

Exercise 2
Mendelian Genetics

Objectives

1. Obtain an Understanding of Dominant verses Recessive Traits
2. Obtain an Understanding of Genetic Linkage and Recombination
3. Obtain an Understanding of Segregation and Independent Assortment

Introduction

One of the easiest ways to see how genes transfer from parent to child is through experimentation. While we can study human traits by studying ancestry, it is neither feasible nor ethical to test-cross human beings just to see how specific traits are passed from parent to child. Additionally, the length of time necessary for such experimentation is far beyond what would work in a laboratory setting. For these reasons along with the moral obligation we have as scientists, we seek answers to inheritance and other genetic questions through the use of model organisms.

Model organisms are microorganisms, animals, or plants that can be used to study a variety of questions (2). In this laboratory exercise you will begin by evaluating Drosophila as your model organism. A common fruit fly, these organisms have a rapid reproductive rate, can be selectively mated to study a wide variety of traits and enable evaluation of a wide range of human concerns including host-pathogen interactions (3).

Trait	Specific Options
Gender	Male or Female
Bristles	Wildtype, Forked, Shaven, Singed, Spineless, or Stubble
Body Color	Wildtype, Black, Ebony, Sable, Tan, or Yellow
Antennae	Wildtype or Aristapedia
Eye Color	Wildtype (Red), Brown, Purple, Sepia, or White
Eye Shape	Wildtype, Bar, Eyeless, Lobe, or Star
Wing Size	Wildtype, Apterous (Wingless), Miniature, or Vestigial
Wing Shape	Wildtype, Curly, Curved, Dumpy, or Scalloped
Wing Vein	Wildtype, Crossveinless, or Incomplete
Wing Angle	Wildtype or Dichaete

When studying inheritance it is best to start with easily visualized traits that follow traditional Mendelian inheritance patterns. Many of the traits listed in the chart above are clearly discernable on the organism as they generate distinct physical features.

Key Terminology:
Genotype = genetic make-up
Phenotype = physical appearance
Recessive Trait = requires both copies of a gene to confer the associated phenotype
Dominant Trait = requires only one copy of a gene to confer the associated phenotype
Autosomal = derived from a gene located on one of the autosomes
Sex-linked = derived from a gene located on one of the sex chromosomes

As direct manipulation of model organisms can be cost or space prohibitive, there are several different virtual programs and simulations that can be utilized to evaluate the key concepts of Mendelian Inheritance. If model organisms are not available, an appropriate, alternative option will be chosen for your utilization in this experiment. Regardless of the program selected, this lab requires a great deal of personal commitment and initiative to be successful. You will get out of it what you put into it. Take your time with it and attempt multiple parental and offspring crosses. You will have a minimum number of crosses of specific types to perform as part of your assignment. In this class and in life, the minimum is never enough to achieve excellence.

Prior to working with a simulation to demonstrate Mendelian Inheritance, it is important that we understand a few basic concepts. You are likely familiar with Punnett Squares; however, it is important that we focus on the role of these as PREDICTIONS of outcomes based on a HYPOTHESIS. For example, if I believe that a gene is located on an autosome and is recessive, I would state that I hypothesize that the trait is AUTOSOMAL RECESSIVE compared to another trait.

Mendelian Genetics teaches us that traits are inherited as units and that like units separate. We know that traits are encoded by genes and that these genes are organized onto chromosomes. In diploid organisms, we have two copies of each gene with one copy passed down the maternal side and the other from the paternal side. These two copies align and segregate during meiosis yielding a single copy to each daughter cell to form the haploid gametes. We use this knowledge to form the basis of our hypothesis.

In this exercise, you will use a computer program to evaluate key factors in Mendelian Inheritance. You will explore both autosomal and sex-linked traits and define the differences in their inheritance patterns using a hypothesis-driven methodology.

Pre-Laboratory Questions

1. Chose a trait variant from the chart above. Write a hypothesis for how you think that variant is inherited compared to the wildtype variant.

   _____

   _____

   _____

   _____

2. What are the possible GENOTYPES of your choice and what are their correlating PHENOTYPES?

   _____

   _____

   _____

   _____

3. What are the expected ratios of phenotype from a cross between a homozygous wildtype variant and the homozygous fly of your selected variant? Include a Punnett Square in your answer.

   _____

   _____

   _____

   _____

4. You mate two of the offspring from the mating in question #3 (F1 generation). What is the expected ratio for your phenotypes (F2 generation)? Include a Punnett square in your answer.

   _____

   _____

   _____

   _____

5. Imagine that you have completed the crosses you describe in the previous questions. Explain what data you would need to see to achieve support for your hypothesis. Be sure to include hypothetical numbers in this answer.

_____

_____

_____

_____

_____

_____

_____

_____

_____

_____

_____

_____

_____

_____

Additional materials based on the chosen program will be provided. If model organisms are available the following general procedure will be utilized.

Procedure: Mendelian Genetics

Manipulation of living organisms can be difficult and result in complications for both you and the organism. Please be sure to follow all directions as outlined by your instructors during the laboratory session.

The basic procedure for evaluating the outcomes from a cross is as follows:

1. Obtain the appropriate vials of flies from your instructor
2. Anesthetize the flies (see additional instructions provided by your instructor for the specific process to be utilized)
3. Using a dissecting microscope, separate your flies into the various phenotypic categories and by sex
4. Count the number of flies exhibiting a given phenotype and biological sex

Record All Findings in the Space Provided:

Additional Notes and Documentation:

Post-Laboratory Assignment

The post-laboratory assignment is to complete the exercise as outlined in the program or procedure performed. The questions you must submit to your instructor are contained within the specific course in the program. Check with your instructor to verify the specific requirements for your laboratory session.

You should be able to summarize your hypotheses and determine whether or not your results support your initial hypotheses. You may be asked to supply this summary as part of your post-laboratory assignment.

Exercise 3
Cytogenetics Introduction

Objectives

1. Begin to Obtain an Understanding of Chromosomes
2. Obtain an Understanding of Chromosome Condensation during Mitosis

Introduction

Chromosomes = the protein and nucleic acid complex that contains the genetic material

Locus = physical location of a gene on a chromosome

Homologs = the members of a pair of matching chromosomes in a diploid set

Sister chromatids = the 2 copies of the chromosome joined at the centromere; formed after DNA replication during mitosis

Condensation of the genetic material into chromosomes occurs during mitosis and meiosis. This condensation results in increased visibility of the chromosomes enabling scientists to study them. In order to study the chromosomes for more than a few moments, cells must be frozen at the proper stage of cellular division. The chemical we will use in this exercise to "freeze" cells during mitosis is colchicine.

Cytogenetics = the field of genetics involving microscopic examination of chromosomes

Chromosomes are classified by the location of the centromere, size, and banding patterns when stained with dyes. Chromosomes can be classified as metacentric, submetacentric, acrocentric, and telocentric.

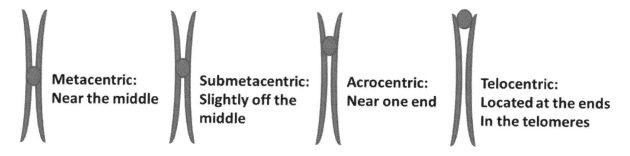

Metacentric: Near the middle

Submetacentric: Slightly off the middle

Acrocentric: Near one end

Telocentric: Located at the ends In the telomeres

In order to visualize chromosomes in this exercise, you will need to stain them. Classical cytogenetics utilizes a range of options and techniques (4). A common stain utilized in chromosome analysis is Giemsa. Additional stains exist to visualize specific chromosomal regions. The method employed is critical to defining the specific structures and contents of the chromosome.

Cytogenetics is more than what it might first appear. The chromosomes can indicate a great deal about the very nature of life. Large scale variations such as changes to chromosome number are visible in cytogenetic analysis. This basic analysis remains a useful diagnostic tool particularly in the diagnosis of leukemia and lymphoma (5). Differential cytogenetic staining can be used to define the specific chromosomal anomalies present in a cell and thus the specific leukemia or lymphoma. The various techniques employed can give a significant amount of information about the type of anomaly present. Common cytogenetic anomalies include: translocations, deletions, duplications, and inversions. Depending on the method of staining, cytogenetic analysis can detect most of the chromosomal anomalies present in a cell.

This exercise will delve into the basic principles of cytogenetic analysis. It will enable you to study differences in chromosome number across different cell lines. The successful completion of this exercise relies heavily on proper treatment of the cells from start to finish. Follow all directions carefully and treat the cells with a gentle hand.

Pre-Laboratory Questions

To answer some of these questions (as well as others throughout this manual), you will have to perform basic internet research. Remember to use SCHOLARLY sources and appropriately cite them.

1. How does Colcemid function to stop cellular division?

   _____
   _____
   _____
   _____
   _____
   _____
   _____
   _____
   _____
   _____
   _____
   _____
   _____
   _____

2. List at least two experimental uses of Giemsa stain.

   _____
   _____
   _____
   _____
   _____

3. What does the term G-banding refer to in regards to chromosomes? How does this type of banding enable scientists to analyze chromosomes?

   _____
   _____
   _____
   _____
   _____
   _____
   _____
   _____
   _____
   _____
   _____
   _____
   _____
   _____

Procedure

A significant amount of preparation is necessary to successfully complete this laboratory exercise. Your instructor will initiate and maintain cell cultures for the cell types that you will study in this exercise. In order to ensure you have enough time to complete the procedure, the starting point for your portion of the exercise may change depending on the time constraints and safety equipment available in your laboratory session. Be sure to listen to your instructor regarding which step should be your first step.

1. Prepare Slides by Pre-Soaking in a 1:1 mix of Ethanol to Hydrochloric Acid (minimum of 1 hour; maximum of overnight)

2. Rinse slides with Distilled Water and maintain in 200 proof Ethanol until needed

3. Add 5 µg/ml Colcemid to Tissue Culture Flasks with cells growing exponentially (Log Phase)

4. Return the cells to culture for 4 to 5 hours minimum

5. Gently swirl the dish to redistribute the cells

6. Transfer the material to a 15 ml centrifuge tube

7. Centrifuge the tube at 1000 rpm for 5 minutes

8. Carefully remove the supernatant from the pellet of cells

9. Loosen the pellet by flicking the tube and resuspoend the pellet in 5 ml hypotonic solution (0.4% KCl) pre-warmed to 37°C mix gently but thoroughly and incubate at 37°C for15 minutes

10. Spin at 1000 rpm for 5 minutes

11. Carefully remove all but 1 ml of supernatant

12. Resuspend the pellet into the remaining liquid by carefully pipetting up and down SLOWLY

13. SLOWLY add 3 ml of iced Carnoy's fixative (1 part glacial acetic acid to 3 parts methanol) shaking the tube very gently (the cells are extremely fragile so handle with care to avoid fragmenting them)

14. Spin at 1000 rpm for 5 minutes

15. Carefully remove most of the fixative leaving only a small amount above the pellet

16. Slowly add 3 ml of fresh fixative to the pellet and resuspend gently

17. Incubate at room temperature for 10 minutes

18. Spin at 1000 rpm for 5 minutes

19. Carefully remove most of the fixative leaving only a small amount above the pellet

20. Slowly add 3 ml of fresh fixative to the pellet and resuspend gently

21. Spin at 1000 rpm for 5 minutes

22. Carefully remove most of the fixative leaving only a small amount above the pellet

23. Slowly add 500 µl of fresh fixative to the pellet and resuspend gently using a pipetman

24. From a distance of approximately 2 inches drop 1 to 2 drops of solution on a clean prepared slide from above

25. Place slide on a slide warmer until completely dry

26. Place slide in slide chamber with 15% Giemsa for 30 minutes (stain will intensify under longer incubations with Giemsa)

27. Remove slide and rinse with water

28. Dry the bottom of the slide and examine under the microscope (you will eventually examine it under oil immersion but only when completely dry)

>   NOTE: NEVER examine a slide on lower power once oil has been added to the slide!

29. Find a metaphase spread of chromosomes and determine the chromosome number (Be sure to note any unique features)

Results

Keep a record of your cell line name and your findings.

Be sure to either photograph or draw documentation of the images you view in the microscope.

Post-Laboratory Assignment

Write a brief RESULTS summary of your chromosome content and appearance. If you were unable to generate metaphase chromosomes, you should explain why the experiment was unsuccessful. Additional assignments may be provided as part of the materials provided by your instructor.

Exercise 4
Chromosome Comparison

Objectives

1. Compare and Contrast Human and Animal Chromosomes
2. Obtain a Greater Understanding of Karyotyping and Its Applications

Introduction

Chromosome number and content is not universal across all species. This exercise is designed to further your understanding of chromosomes and the genetic information they contain. In this exercise you will have the opportunity to compare the chromosome numbers for a variety of animal species to humans. Additionally, you may have an opportunity to perform karyotype analysis using Cytovision™. This analysis will enable you to compare chromosome content across cancer cell lines.

Karyotype = the numerical summary of the chromosome content as defined by the karyogram

Karyogram = the pictorial depiction of chromosome content by size starting with chromosome 1 and ending in the sex chromosomes

One method of analyzing chromosome content involves selectively "painting" chromosomes with fluorescent markers. This procedure known as Fluorescent *in situ* Hybridization, (FISH) can be highly specific and provide a great deal of information regarding the genetic content of a cell or organism.

In this exercise you will have an opportunity to view chromosome spreads stained using a variety of methods. You will be expected to organize chromosome preps using Cytovision™. Cytovision™ is a program capable of analyzing images of preps into the appropriate size and distribution for the organism thus generating the karyogram and is utilized for these evaluations for a wide range of situations including clinically (6). The software must be told what to do so it is important that you know what you are working with prior to initiating the analysis. Be sure to adequately review and research the materials you are given before proceeding with the analysis. Additionally, you will be presented several karyograms to evaluate and define.

Each image or slide will have a corresponding handout with questions. In this exercise you are expected to work in groups of 2 to 4 students and each of you will perform one analysis. You must obtain the data from the other members of your group in order to complete the assignment. Use your best judgment and work together.

Pre-Laboratory Questions

1. How many chromosomes are present in a human cell during typical cellular development? _____

2. How many chromosomes are present in a human cell after S phase of mitosis but prior to cytokinesis? _____

3. Draw a basic karyogram for a normal human male. This does not have to be fancy but make sure it contains the correct number of chromosomes and the correct sex chromosomes.

4. Explain what 47, XXY means. (What is this and what does it tell us?)

_____

_____

_____

_____

_____

_____

Procedure

Your instructor has prepared a series of slides for you to analyze. Additionally you will be given handouts with a variety of karyograms to analyze. You will have the opportunity to use Cytovision™ to analyze the slides in more detail. This will be completed in groups of 2 to 4 students and represents the most time consuming portion of the procedure. Familiarize yourself with some of the program specifics using the handouts provided by your instructor.

1. Review the slides you are given regarding cell type and organism

2. Use the internet to find information pertinent to your analysis such as expected chromosome number and specifics about the staining method indicated on the slide

3. Use Cytovision™ to organize the chromosomes into a karyogram

4. Analyze the FISH slides for positive staining as well

While awaiting your chance to work with the program:

5. You have been given several karyograms. These should take a significant amount of time to review and analyze so work together as much as possible

6. Determine the organism represented by each karyogram and answer all questions provided in the handouts. If the karyogram represents a human cell, determine the karyotype and diagnosis. Each table has a different set to analyze so please remain in your individual groups of 2 to 4 students.

Results and Post Laboratory Assignment

The majority of this lab involves recording your observations and findings. Use the following page to make notations regarding your findings and draw pertinent images for your notebook. Answer the assigned questions from your handouts.

RESULTS

Exercise 5
DNA Extraction and Analysis

Objectives

1. Obtain an Understanding of DNA Extraction Techniques
2. Learn How to Determine DNA Quality and Quantity

Introduction

There are several protocols for extracting DNA for a multitude of purposes (7-9). The first step to any extraction involves lysing the cells to release the DNA. A general lysis buffer is going to contain both an agent that breaks open the cells and a buffering agent to preserve/protect the DNA. The quality of these components is a major contributor to the quality of DNA. Old or low quality components will result in low DNA yields.

Basic Lysis Buffer Components:
100mM EDTA
10 mM Tris (pH 7.5)
1% SDS (detergent to lyse cells)
water

Once the cell is lysed, DNA must be adequately sheared to ensure fragments small enough for further analysis. If whole DNA is desired other protocols must be followed. The main component of extracted material from the cells is protein. Protein is a major source of contamination for DNA and can significantly affect reactions. By including proteinase K, an enzyme that degrades proteins, the level of protein can be reduced and the quality of DNA improved. Additionally, homogenization and adequate DNA shearing are essential to high yields of high quality DNA. Carefully balancing caution and strength is critical to the overall outcomes.

The procedure outlined in this exercise is based on a kit optimized to produce excellent yields of DNA for further analysis via polymerase chain reaction (PCR). Several of the components are commercially available in a single kit including the spin columns and collection tubes. Purchasing these components ensures they are certified DNase, RNase, and contaminant free.

Determining the concentration and purity of your DNA sample is a relatively simple process. The concentration of DNA can be determined by the following formula:

$$\text{Concentration} = 50\ \mu g/ml \times A260 \times \text{dilution factor}$$
Where A260 is the level of light absorbance at a wavelength of 260 nm

By analyzing the ratio of absorbances at 260nm over 280 nm (A260/A280), we can ascertain the presence of contaminants such as protein. Pure DNA results in a value of 1.8 to 2.0 for this ratio. It is important to note that there are several factors which can alter this value. For example, the ratio will decrease as pH decreases (10). It is therefore necessary to consider what buffer is used when determining the concentrations. Typically we use water or a simple Tris buffer at a pH of 7.5.

As technologies have improved, the means through which we can analyze DNA concentration and quality have evolved. While comparisons of absorbance remain a gold standard of evaluation, additional methods can be utilized to define DNA content and assess purity particularly in clinical settings for analysis of cell-free DNA (7). In this exercise you will extract DNA and determine the concentration of the samples. You will then save these samples for further analysis. It is essential that you exercise caution when performing these steps. Contamination of your sample will affect your results now and in future experiments that require these samples.

Pre-Laboratory Questions

1. List three potential contaminants of your DNA and explain how each would affect the outcomes you're your extraction.

   _____

   _____

   _____

   _____

   _____

   _____

   _____

   _____

   _____

2. Explain why DNA is considered to be stable and can be manipulated at room temperature.

   _____

   _____

   _____

   _____

   _____

   _____

3. Determine the DNA concentrations for the following absorbance results and explain what they mean:

	A260	A280
Sample 1	0.329	0.176
Sample 2	0.317	0.154
Sample 3	0.455	0.246
Sample 4	1.63	0.052

   _____

   _____

   _____

   _____

   _____

   _____

   _____

   _____

   _____

   _____

   _____

   _____

Procedure

1. Thaw cell pellets on ice until the pellet can easily be dislodged from the bottom of the microcentrifuge tube

2. Add 200 µl 1X PBS to each sample

3. Add 20 µl of Proteinase K to eah sample

4. Mix thoroughly via vortexing

5. Incubate at room temperature for 5 minutes

6. Add 200 µl Buffer 1 to each sample

7. Vigorously mix- must be severely mixed to properly shear DNA

8. Incubate at 56°C for 10 minutes

9. Add 200 µl ethanol to each sample

10. Mix thoroughly via vortexing

11. Transfer the solution to one spin column with collection tube attached per sample

12. Centrifuge the tubes at 8000 rpm for 1 minute

13. Discard the flow through, tap the collection tube briefly to dry, and re-insert the spin column into the collection tube

14. Add 500 µl Buffer 2 to each sample

15. Centrifuge the tubes at 8000 rpm for 1 minute

16. Discard the flow through, tap the collection tube briefly to dry, and re-insert the spin column into the collection tube

17. Add 500 µl Buffer 3 to each sample

18. Centrifuge the tubes at 8000 rpm for 1 minute

19. Discard the flow through, tap the collection tube briefly to dry, and re-insert the spin column into the collection tube

20. Centrifuge the tubes at 14,000 rpm for 2 minutes

21. Discard the collection tube with flow through and insert spin column into a fresh collection tube

22. Add 200 µl Buffer 4 (elution buffer) to each sample

23. Incubate at room temperature for 1 minute

24. Centrifuge the tubes at 8000 rpm for 1 minute

25. Transfer the flow through into a microcentrifuge tube (recovery tube)

26. Transfer 20 µl from the recovery tube into a separate microcentrifuge tube for analysis of DNA concentration and transfer the original recovery tube to ice

Analysis of DNA Concentration and Purity

There are a variety of methods for the analysis of DNA concentration. The method outlined below represents a generic evaluation using a basic spectrophotometer. Additional options may be available that will alter this portion of the experiment. Please be sure to follow the directions provided by your instructor.

1. Add 180 µl TE buffer to the aliquot of DNA for a final volume of 200 µl

2. Add 100 µl of the mixture to each of two cuvettes containing 900 µl of TE buffer; prepare 1 cuvette with 1000 µl of TE Buffer

3. Use the blank sample (TE Buffer only) to establish the baseline for the machine

4. Read the absorbance of the DNA sample at 230 nm, 260 nm, and 280 nm for each cuvette

Results

NOTE: These results may need to be edited to match your specific samples. Use the space provided as a guideline.

Standard 1 read 1: _____   Standard 1 read 2: _____

Standard 2 read 1: _____   Standard 2 read 2: _____

Unknown 1 read 1:_____   Unknown 1 read 2:_____

Unknown 2 read 1:_____   Unknown 2 read 2:_____

Use the space below to record additional results and observations.

Post-Laboratory Assignment

Write a brief paragraph regarding your results. This should be less than one double-spaced page and include any conclusions you are able to make at the end of the exercise. Part of this assignment is to understand what your results are and how to draw conclusions from them. Be sure to provide context for your results by including a statement introducing the main goal and at least one potential future direction for the research.

Exercise 6
Evaluating DNA via PCR and Gel Electrophoresis

Objectives

1. Compare and Contrast Animal and Human DNA
2. Obtaining an Understanding of Polymerase Chain Reaction
3. Learn to Analyze DNA and Genetic Content

Introduction

Extraction and analysis of DNA composition is a relatively simple process. Several molecular tools exist to enable highly-specific scientific inquiry and investigation. Even minute amounts of genetic material can be analyzed if the proper tools are available. Through the use of polymerase chain reaction (PCR), we can amplify specific sequences of DNA for further analysis. PCR utilizes primers complementary to specific genomic sequences to initiate replication of highly-specific fragments of DNA. Through repeated rounds of replication, a significant amount of material can be generated.

Multiple cycles of strand separation (denaturation), primer annealing, and extension of new material, lead to several thousand copies of a gene of interest; enough to visualize the genetic material on a gel. The image below outlines the general steps of the reaction. DNA denaturation and strand extension are set at the melting point for DNA and the optimal temperature for the strand extension, respectively.

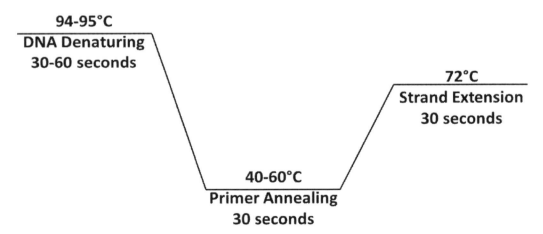

Figure 1. Basic Steps and Temperatures of PCR.

As seen in the image below, the number of fragments generated rapidly increases with each cycle.

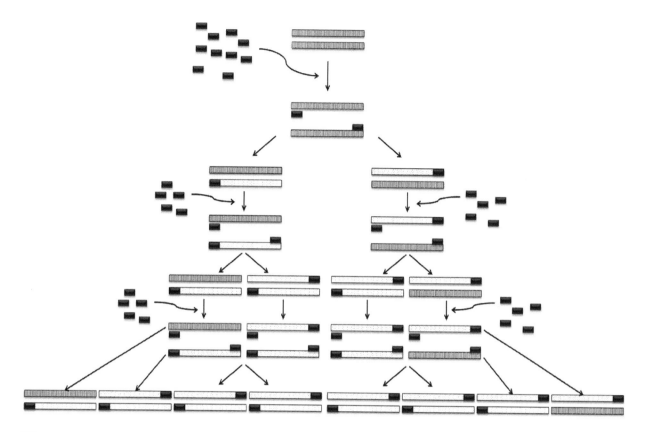

Figure 2. Basic PCR Primer Binding and Product Formation. The black boxes represent primers (both forward and reverse) and the long rectangles represent DNA.

Each component in the reaction mixture serves an important purpose. As with cooking, low quality ingredients make for a low quality final product.

Components:

    Water
    PCR Buffer
    Deoxynucleotide triphosphates (dNTPs)
    MgCl2
    Forward Primer
    Reverse Primer
    Taq Polymerase
    DNA

DNA is perhaps the most obvious ingredient though it can be a source of difficulty for some reactions. Too much starting material can cause poor reactivity as can too little. Additionally, the DNA must be of good quality and without contamination from other sources including other DNA sources.

In order to produce the new DNA fragments, raw material must be present in the reaction mix. We add dNTPs to the mix to serve as the raw material. It contains the 4 nucleotides required to produce the new DNA fragments. Additionally these dNTPs provide the energy necessary to complete the PCR reaction.

Water serves as the material necessary to generate the liquid environment that permits the reaction to occur. It is the matrix in which the PCR components interact. Although it seems to be the most basic component, It often poses the greatest source of aggravation as contamination and consistency are often an issue. To solve this problem, treated water that is certified contaminant free is typically purchased.

The primers act as both the site of reaction initiation and as the source or reaction specificity (see Figure 2). These can be personally designed against specific sequences or commercially available primers can be purchased. These primers are oligonucleotides. Both a forward and a reverse primer must be used to generate the desired fragments.

Oligonucleotides = short, synthetic, single-stranded DNA segments complementary to the DNA sequence flanking the region to be amplified

The PCR buffer serves to provide the appropriate pH and salt environment for optimal reactivity. MgCl2 is often already included in this buffer. MgCl2 is important as it provides the cations required as a cofactor for the taq polymerase. This is the most variable ingredient as its concentration can be altered to optimize the reaction.

Taq polymerase is the final ingredient and is responsible for catalyzing the PCR reaction and strand extension. Taq polymerase, originally identified in bacteria thermophiles, is utilized in this system because it has the ability to withstand high temperatures. Its optimal temperature for activity is roughly 72°C so strand extension is typically set to that temperature.

Once the fragments have been produced it is possible to separate them by size and visualize the DNA using gel electrophoresis. In order to actually see the unique bands produced, we use an agent that glows when exposed to UV light, the DNA-intercalating agent, ethidium bromide (EtBr). The EtBr is incorporated into the gel and interacts with the DNA fragments following the electrophoresis. The interaction causes the DNA to fluoresce in response to UV light. We can then capture an image of the gel and analyze the resulting bands.

Pre-Laboratory Questions

1. What mathematic formula represents the number of DNA fragments after each cycle? _____

2. How many fragments of DNA are produced by 5 rounds of PCR from a single original fragment? _____

3. How many fragments of DNA are produced by 30 rounds of PCR from a single original fragment? _____

4. You realize after you complete your PCR that you forgot to include an ingredient in the master mix applied to half of your samples (samples 3 and 4). Based on your results below, what ingredient did you fail to include? Explain your answer.

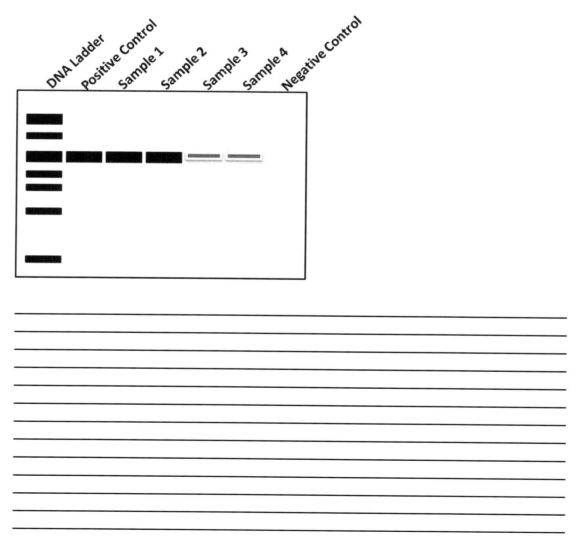

_____
_____
_____
_____
_____
_____
_____
_____
_____
_____
_____
_____
_____

Part A
Polymerase Chain Reaction

Noteworthy Information

Stephen Covey once said, "I am not a product of my circumstances; I am a product of my decisions."

This study is all about the circumstances created by specific decisions. It relies heavily on an ability to avoid contamination and exercise caution. Your decisions will determine the success of this exercise. Follow the instructions and never assume that just because something is relatively short and simple that it is, in any way, "easy".

Procedure

1. Carefully pipet 2 µl of DNA into the PCR reaction tubes or plate

    Avoid touching the tip to the sides of the wells and only pipet directly into the bottom of each well

2. Prepare your master mix ON ICE as follows per sample
    You will need to calculate how much of each ingredient you need to complete the entire experiment;
    Use the formula: $n + 2$ to determine the number of mixes you need
    Where n = the number of samples you are analyzing including all controls
    a. Water   16.8 µl
    b. PCR Buffer (10X)   2.5 µl
    c. dNTPs (8mM)   2.5 µl
    d. forward primer (10 µM)   1.2 µl
    e. reverse primer (10 µM)   1.2 µl
    f. taq polymerase   0.03 µl
3. Mix thoroughly via gentle flicking (vortexing can heat the mix too much)
4. Carefully pipet 23 µl of mix onto your DNA
5. Spin the wells or plate to disperse the reaction mix into the DNA

6. Place the reaction tubes or plate into a pre-warmed thermocycler and initiate the PCR reaction (Be sure to note the specifics of your cycle in the space below)
7. The products must be kept at 4°C following completion of the reaction; keep on ice or transfer to the fridge until ready to move on with the analysis

Use the space below to record important details and observations.

Part B
Gel Electrophoresis

Noteworthy Information

"I've learned that people will forget what you said, people will forget what you did, but people will never forget how you made them feel."— Maya Angelou

In Science, it is important that you neither forget what you said nor what you did. These are major factors to successful science. Knowing what you did in your experiment and being able to present those results to a broad audience are essential skills. Data analysis is just the first step to communicating your findings. You must then be able to tell us what those results mean.

Procedure

8. Prepare an agarose gel by mixing 1.25 g Agarose powder with 125 ml TAE buffer

9. Melt the solution by microwaving briefly until clear

10. Allow it to cool then add 10 µl Ethidium Bromide to the solution prior to it solidifying but after it has cooled significantly

11. Pour the mixture into the gel box and insert combs to generate wells

12. Mix the PCR product mixture with 6 µl loading buffer

13. Remove the gel combs and transfer the gel to the electrophoresis box and fill the box with TAE buffer until gel is covered with 2 to 3 mm of buffer

    Be sure the gel is loaded so the wells can RUN to RED

14. Transfer half of the sample into the wells of the solid gel leaving the first well empty

15. Load 10 µl of DNA ladder to the first well of the gel

16. Run the gel at 100V until the dye approaches the end of the gel

17. Evaluate the gel using the UV light box available in the laboratory

Post-Laboratory Assignment

Prepare a brief summary of your results (less than 1 double-spaced page). Be sure to address the following questions in your summary:
1. What conclusions can you draw from your results?
2. Are there any differences in your samples compared to the controls?
3. Did you include all of the appropriate controls to draw conclusions?
4. What your PCR successful or was there contamination? How do you know?

Exercise 7
Plasmid Isolation

Objectives

1. Isolate Plasmids for Bacterial Transformations
2. Re-enforce Your Understanding of Basic Fluorometry and its Applications

Introduction

Extracting plasmid DNA requires retention of the entire, unaltered genetic material. As such, traditional DNA extraction techniques cannot be used. The early steps of the two protocols are similar in that the cell must be rendered capable of releasing the DNA; however, the type of buffer used and the overall handling differ significantly. For instance, in whole plasmid extraction, it is essential to buffer the reaction to protect the plasmid DNA. As such, the cell is rendered more permeable as opposed to being fully lysed in the early stages of the procedure.

Reaction Ingredient	Function
0.2M NaOH/1% SDS	Permeabilizes the cells and denatures the nucleases, chromosomal DNA and linear plasmids
3M Potassium Acetate (KOAc)	neutralizing step- stops the detergent reaction and precipitates the chromosomal DNA, cellular debris, and SDS
Isopropyl Alcohol	Precipitates the plasmid DNA
Glucose-Tris-EDTA Buffer (GTE)	Buffers the reaction and helps prevent the shearing or denaturing of plasmid DNA; disrupts the outer membrane without fully lysing the cell

The careful, stepwise addition of these ingredients results in significant plasmid DNA yields. This isolated plasmid DNA can then be used to transform bacteria and produce large amounts of a desired protein. In order to perform future studies with the plasmid, you must also determine the amount of plasmid present in your sample. Since the plasmid we are using contains a protein that fluoresces under UV light, green fluorescent protein (GFP), we can measure the amount of plasmid via fluorometry. This measures the level of fluorescent light produced by the sample. By comparing the readouts for known concentrations of plasmid to your unknown samples, we can define the concentration of plasmid in your sample.

Pre-Laboratory Questions

1. You measure your 50 µg/ml standard DNA on the fluorometer and obtain a reading of 100. After reading your sample, you obtain a reading of 125. What is the concentration of your sample? _____

2. You got distracted and accidently left your sample at room temperature following addition of the NaOH/SDS mixture. What might this mean for your sample?

   _____
   _____
   _____
   _____
   _____
   _____

3. You once again got distracted and accidently left your NaOH/SDS mixture on your bacteria for 30 minutes. What might this mean for your sample?

   _____
   _____
   _____
   _____
   _____
   _____

4. Once again, you allowed distractions to affect you and left your sample out for 15 minutes at room temperature following addition of the isopropyl alcohol. What might this mean for your sample?

   _____
   _____
   _____
   _____
   _____
   _____

Part A
Plasmid Isolation

Noteworthy Information

Isolating plasmid DNA is a relatively straightforward process. The goal is to isolate the DNA in its entirety as opposed to isolating fragmented DNA or chromosomal preps outlined in previous experiments. The plasmids isolated from this step can be used to transform bacteria and generate additional plasmid DNA.

For many of these steps to work, the solutions must be relatively fresh. This is particularly important for the sodium dilaurel sulfate (SDS). This detergent has been shown to exhibit reduced efficacy over time in suspension. Additionally, like all procedures that require incubation on ice, it is critical that you keep the cold solutions cold and avoid excessive handling or heat.

Procedure

1. Grow bacteria cultures containing plasmid DNA overnight
2. Transfer cultures to centrifuge bottles and centrifuge for 10 minutes at 7000 rpm and 4°C using the Sorvall Centrifuge
3. Remove supernatant and re-suspend pellets in 4 ml GTE buffer
4. Transfer mix to 50 ml centrifuge tubes and store at -20°C until needed (1 tube per 2 to 4 students)
5. Add 4 ml 0.2M NaOH/1%SDS mixture
6. Mix thoroughly via vortexing and incubate for 10 minutes on ice (the solution should thicken and become clear)
7. Add 3 ml 3M KOAc at pH 5.5
8. Mix thoroughly via vortexing and incubate for 10 minutes on ice (until a white precipitate forms)
9. During the incubations, label 20 microcentrifuge tubes with your initials
10. Transfer to the series of microcentrifuge tubes and centrifuge for 10 minutes at 12,000 rpm and 25°C
11. Filter the supernatant through gauze into a 50 ml centrifuge tube
12. Add 4 ml isopropyl alcohol to the mixture

13. Incubate the mix for 5 minutes at room temperature

14. Transfer to microcentrifuge tubes (make sure you use an even number and fill the tubes with equal volumes)

15. Centrifuge the tubes for 10 minutes at 12,000 rpm and 25°C

16. Discard supernatant and dissolve pellet in 250 µl GTE buffer one tube at a time (keep transferring the full volume to the next tube until all pellets are dissolved and combined in one tube; transfer the full volume to a new tube labeled PLASMID DNA and your initials)

17. Transfer 6 µl of samples to another microcentrifuge tube and set aside

18. Add 5 µl of RNase A (20 mg/ml) to the labeled tube and keep on ice

19. Take the 6 µl tube you prepared to determine the concentration of plasmid in your sample (see Part B: Fluorometry)

Part B
Fluorometry

Noteworthy Information

Once you have the plasmid DNA, in order for it to be utilized in experimentation, you must know how much you obtained. Determining the concentration is a relatively simple process though does vary slightly from the previous method. In this portion of the experiment you will utilize a fluorometer to measure the DNA concentration. The samples will need to be diluted in H-stain solution (2M LiCl, 50 mM Tris pH 7.5, and 10 µl/ml H33258).

Procedure

1. Be sure the fluorometer is turned on for 15 minutes prior to initiating experiment

2. Add 1.5 ml H-stain solution to 4 cuvettes to rinse cuvettes

3. Aspirate solution and add 1.5 ml fresh H-solution to each cuvette

4. Place 1 cuvette into fluorometer and set zero reading (this sets your blank or no DNA reading)

5. Remove cuvette and add 2 µl DNA standard to it and one additional cuvette and mix well

6. To the remaining two cuvettes add 2 µl of your unknown sample

7. Read all four cuvettes twice each

8. Calculate the concentration of DNA for your sample

9. Dilute sample in GTE buffer until it is set to a concentration of 50 ng/µl

10. Store plasmid at -20°C

Results

Standard 1 read 1: _____   Standard 1 read 2: _____

Standard 2 read 1: _____   Standard 2 read 2: _____

Unknown 1 read 1:_____   Unknown 1 read 2:_____

Unknown 2 read 1:_____   Unknown 2 read 2:_____

Post-Laboratory Assignment

Write a brief paragraph regarding your results. This should be less than one double-spaced page and include any conclusions you are able to make at the end of the exercise. Part of this assignment is knowing what your results are and how to draw conclusions from them. Be sure to provide context for your results by including at least one potential future direction for the research.

Exercise 8
Plasmid Evaluation via Restriction Digestion

Objectives

1. Apply the Principles of a Restriction Digest to Plasmid Analysis
2. Review the Applications of Restriction Enzymes in Genetics and Recombinant DNA

Introduction

Restriction Enzymes = enzymes that cut DNA at specific recognition sequences called "sites".

In general, restriction enzymes are ENDONUCLEASES that recognize 4 to 8 base regions of DNA. (Endonucleases = enzymes that cut DNA within a strand rather than at an end). All restriction enzyme sites are palindromes. For example, the Eco RI restriction enzyme recognizes the site 5'GAATTC3' (with the complementary sequence of the other strand being 3'CTTAAG5'). ANY place this sequence appears in the DNA, Eco RI will cut it.

EcoRI site: 5'—G-A-A-T-T-C—3'
            3'—C-T-T-A-A-G—5'

Restriction Mapping = utilizing a series of restriction enzymes to digest (cut) DNA and then separating fragments via gel electrophoresis.

Gel Electrophoresis = running a current across a matrix to produce a charge differential capable of separating material

DNA is negatively charged and will move through a matrix toward the positive electrode. The pattern of bands and sizes of fragments following restriction digestion and gel electrophoresis can be used to get information about an unknown piece of DNA or to confirm expected results following transformation. By utilizing commercially available or "known" plasmids with "known" cut/restriction sites, you can determine whether an unknown segment contains any sequences recognized by restriction enzymes. Therefore, by using multiple enzymes, we can determine the structure/sequence of a piece of DNA.

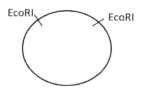

Consider the image to the left. How many pieces/fragments of DNA would be produced if the plasmid were cut with EcoRI? Use the diagram to the left to answer the question. This diagram is a basic plasmid map. On the plasmid map, there are 2 EcoRI sites indicated. The sites are arranged so that 2

63

fragments would be produced. The 2 pieces would be different sizes and would separate during gel electrophoresis to different positions in a gel.

These principles are true regardless of the type or number of restriction enzymes utilized. In fact, using a combination of enzymes can give significant information about the sequence of the plasmid.

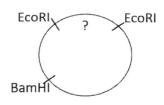

Consider this image on the left. How many pieces/fragments of DNA would be produced if the plasmid were cut with EcoRI only? BamHI only? Both EcoRI and BamHI?

There is only one EcoRI site so only 1 fragment would be produced. There are 2 BamHI sites so 2 fragments would be produced. The two combined will produce three fragments with two fragments that are very similar in size. The utilization of unique combinations and cut points does more than just create more fragments. It also enables specificity and unique sequence combinations when generating new plasmids.

It is important to note that when fragments are similar in size they will appear in approximately the same location on the gel after gel electrophoresis. Closely related fragments can be separated by increasing the percentage of agarose in the gel to change the density of the matrix. Fragments of identical size will require further analysis to definitively draw conclusions about the plasmid DNA.

Restriction digestions can be used to give you information about an unknown segment of DNA if you know enough about the plasmid map.

The plasmid to the left is 5kb in size containing an unknown segment of DNA 2 kb in size. When this plasmid contains a known 2 kb insert lacking an EcoRI site and is cut with EcoRI, it produces two fragments of DNA; one 2 kb and one 3 kb in size. BamHI has only one cut site and therefore produces a fragment 5 kb in size (see diagram). Although this information pertains to a known 2 kb insert, we can use this information to define our unknown.

If, for instance, following digestion with EcoRI, we see 4 bands in our gel, we know there is an EcoRI cut site in the unknown segment. The unknown is located between the two original EcoRI sites so a single additional site in the unknown segment will result in 4 pieces. Additional sites will yield additional fragments of various sizes.

If, for instance, following digestion with BamHI, we see 2 bands in our gel, we know there is a BamHI cut site in the unknown segment. Based on the sizes of the new fragments we can define where in the segment of DNA the cut sites are located. We have "mapped" the new EcoRI and BamHI sites.

Pre-Laboratory Questions

1. Perform an internet search for a commercially available plasmid and fill in the following information:
    a. Plasmid Name _____
    b. Company Name _____
    c. List 3 Restriction Sites that can be utilized to cut the plasmid
        i. _____
        ii. _____
        iii. _____
    d. Provide the reference for the plasmid and its design:

    _____

2. The plasmid below has several known restriction enzyme sites (indicated by name).

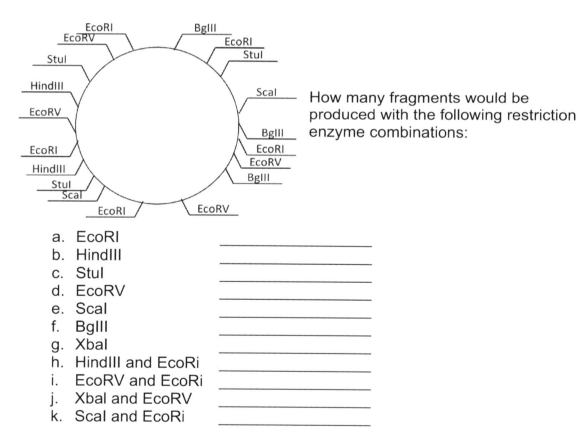

How many fragments would be produced with the following restriction enzyme combinations:

    a. EcoRI _____
    b. HindIII _____
    c. StuI _____
    d. EcoRV _____
    e. ScaI _____
    f. BglII _____
    g. XbaI _____
    h. HindIII and EcoRi _____
    i. EcoRV and EcoRi _____
    j. XbaI and EcoRV _____
    k. ScaI and EcoRi _____

Procedure

1. Label Microcentrifuge tubes: 1 Sample Tube and 1 Control Tube
2. Add 5 µl of Buffer 3.1 to the two tubes
3. Add 5 µl of plasmid DNA at a concentration of 50 ng/µl to the two tubes
4. Add the following to the tubes:
   a. SAMPLE = 8 µl water and

      2 µl of the prepared restriction enzyme mix (20 kU/ml of each restriction enzyme at a 1:1 ratio)
   b. CONTROL = 10 µl water
5. Mix the two tubes via vortexing for 30 seconds
6. Incubate the tubes at 37°C for 15 minutes
7. Add 4 µl loading buffer to the samples
8. Prepare DNA ladder by mixing 1 µl of 1 kb ladder with 19 µl water and 3 µl loading dye
9. Prepare E-Gel by removing the comb and placing it in the electrophoresis chamber
10. Carefully load 20 µl of the ladder, sample, and control to individual wells in the gel (only 1 ladder is needed per gel)
11. Run the gel for 30 to 45 minutes
12. Examine the gel under UV light and photograph it
13. Place the gel in a sealable sandwich bag and add a small amount of TAE buffer
14. Store at 4°C

Results and Post-Laboratory Assignment

In a short paragraph (less than 1 page double-spaced), explain the findings indicated by your gel image. Include a figure of the gel complete with figure legend. If no such image is available, diagram what you would have expected with positive and negative results.

Exercise 9
Transformation

Objectives

1. Obtain an Understanding of the Principles of Bacterial Transformation
2. Learn Aseptic Technique

Introduction

Transformation = the process of inserting foreign DNA into a cell

Plasmids are small circular pieces of DNA that can be made to contain specific genetic material. In order to differentiate transformed bacteria from non-transformed bacteria, these plasmids often contain genes to confer antibiotic resistance to the bacteria or other genetic traits that can easily be differentiated. A common choice for easy, visual conformation of transformation is the presence or absence of fluorescent markers such as green fluorescent protein (GFP). This protein, originally discovered in jellyfish, causes the bacteria to fluoresce when exposed to ultraviolet light (UV).

Bacteria most likely developed the ability to transfer genetic information via plasmids as a means to protect themselves from environmental toxins produced by other organisms such as molds and fungi.

All commercially available plasmids contain:
1. A selectable marker = a means to differentiate transformed bacteria from non-transformed bacteria (typically an antibiotic resistance gene)
    a. AmpR = ampicillin resistance cassette
    b. araC = arabinose operator- controls the transcription of genes under the control of the promoter
2. An origin of replication = a starting point for the bacteria to make more copies of the plasmid (ori; see below)
3. A multiple cloning site = a site containing multiple restriction digest sites for insertion of the gene of interest (gene of interest here is GFP)

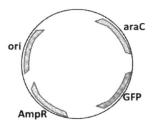

In this exercise, the plasmid that will be utilized contains GFP under control of an arabinose promoter as well as and ampicillin resistance cassette. The image to the left demonstrates the generic set-up for the plasmid though it should be noted that the image is NOT to scale.

Since DNA is highly hydrophilic, it does NOT readily pass through the highly hydrophobic plasma membrane. In order to take-up the plasmid, cells must be made competent or altered to make them capable of letting the DNA into them. This is accomplished by altering the membrane. By punching "holes" in the membrane you create areas where DNA can freely enter the cell. Solutions high in calcium chloride are capable of generating the holes while a series of incubations from on ice to heat (heat-shock) to on ice again can be utilized to force the DNA into the cells. The chloride ions enter the cells and bring H_2O along with them causing the cells to swell. It is important to note that, much like people, cells do not enjoy having their protective barrier punctured using any means. Therefore, cells must be carefully handled and prepared for competency. This preparation serves to maximize both the uptake of DNA and the survival of the bacteria.

We can measure the efficacy of many steps in the process. For instance, the level of cell competency can be calculated based on amount of DNA added and number of colonies that result. To calculate the competency of your cells, divide the number of colonies on your plate by the amount of DNA (in µg) you added to the cells. We can also calculate the relative number of bacteria transformed compared to controls, or transformation efficiency.

Selection = the process of determining which cells have taken up the foreign DNA

By utilizing plasmids that confer antibiotic resistance to sensitive bacteria, the uptake of plasmid DNA can easily be identified. Following transformation the bacteria can be plated on agar plates containing the antibiotic (whose resistance is conferred by the plasmid) and evaluated. This selective growth media enables only bacteria containing resistance to the antibiotic to grow on the plate. Thus, it serves as a means to both identify and isolate the transformed bacteria. Many plasmids contain multiple selectable markers such as genes for both arabinose utilization and resistance to ampicillin. This allows for identification of recombinant plasmids when inserted desired genes into the vectors. One week prior to the laboratory session, you will be given detailed information about the plasmid(s) to be used in the experiment as it may vary depending on availability.

In order to work with bacterial cultures and ensure that the final product is what you actually wanted to grow, certain sanitary precautions must be taken. These precautions are known collectively as aseptic technique. This is not sterile technique as sterile implies absolutely zero microbial growth and we are attempting to grow transformed bacteria.

Aseptic technique requires both careful preparation of the laboratory space and the working materials. Gloves should be worn at all times. All surfaces should be cleaned with ethanol. All materials should be flamed or be sterilized via autoclaving prior to use. Aseptic technique also involves minimal contact with the materials. All tubes and vials should only be held and/or handled with the thumb and forefinger. Additional instructions will be provided as needed to ensure safety and compliance.

Pre-laboratory Questions

1. What is the main difference between competency and transformation efficiency?

   _____
   _____
   _____
   _____
   _____

2. What solution are we using to render our bacteria competent? List all components and define which component is the most important for this process.

   _____
   _____
   _____
   _____
   _____
   _____
   _____
   _____
   _____
   _____

3. A scientist added 10 ng of DNA to a set of cells and wound up with 10^6 colonies on her selection plate. What is the competency of the cells?

   _____
   _____
   _____

4. Define the term "heat-shock".

   _____
   _____
   _____
   _____
   _____
   _____

5. How would you calculate transformation efficiency for your bacteria?

   _____
   _____
   _____
   _____
   _____
   _____

Procedure

This experiment is fully scalable. You may be asked at the beginning to make changes to enable you to perform this experiment on a larger or smaller scale. Be sure to follow all directions provided by your instructor.

1. Aliquot bacteria cultures into pre-chilled 50 ml tubes

2. Incubate on ice for 5 to 10 minutes

3. Centrifuge at 2000 rpm for 5 minutes

4. Suspend each pellet in 10 ml $CaCl_2$ solution

5. Centrifuge at 2000 rpm for 5 minutes

6. Suspend pellet in 2 ml ice-cold $CaCl_2$

7. Aliquot into microcentrifuge tubes and store at -70°C

8. Rapidly warm 2 aliquots of competent cells in your hands

9. Label 1 tube + and 1 tube – (the + tube will be transformed with plasmid)

10. Add 10 µl of purified plasmid to the + tube

11. Mix and place on ice for 10 minutes

12. Transfer cells to 42C for 2 minutes (Heat Shock)

13. Add 1 ml of LB broth to each tube of cells

14. Incubate at 37°C for 15 minutes

15. Streak 4 plates

    a. Transfer 40 µl from (+) tube onto LB-Agar

    b. Transfer 40 µl from (+) tube onto LB/AMP/Ara-Agar plate

    c. Transfer 40 µl from (-) tube onto LB-Agar

    d. Transfer 40 µl from (-) tube onto LB/AMP/Ara-Agar plate

16. Culture at 37°C overnight (plate can be stored at 4°C)

Post-Laboratory Assignment

Results will be posted or provided once available. You will be expected to critically evaluate the outcomes of the experiment and explain any potential deviations in expectations. Write a one page report describing your results. Be sure to include what the expectations were for a successful experiment and explain any deviations in the experiment that you observed.

Exercise 10:
Introduction to Gene Editing via CRISPR

Objectives

1. Evaluate and explain the process of modern gene editing
2. Introduce CRISPR technology and its application
3. Understand and explain the uses and limitations of modern gene editing

Introduction

This laboratory exercise introduces key concepts in modern genetic manipulation. Clustered Regularly Interspaced Short Palindromic Repeats (CRISPR) represent a type of immune protection in bacteria that let the bacterium destroy invading plasmid DNA and viruses (11). There is even a type of memory to this activity as short DNA sequences referred to as spacers from invading viruses can be incorporated at CRISPR loci within the bacterial genome after an initial infection. Once this occurs, reinfection triggers a response in the form of complementary CRISPR RNA matching the DNA sequence and enabling the CRISPR-associated (CAS) nuclease to cleave the DNA forming a double strand break in the foreign DNA. This CRISPR-CAS system has been developed into a gene editing tool that can generate gene knockins, point mutations, and gene knockouts. For more information on the specifics of how this process works, please refer to the posted videos and materials associated with the section.

For this laboratory exercise, you will be using CRISPR-CAS to inhibit gene activity. This additional activity is possible because CRISPR can be used as a targeted delivery system. Cas9 has the ability to bind target DNA without inducing DNA cleavage because the two functions are separate and independent. Alterations to Cas9 in combination with RNAs capable of targeting transcriptional start sites, enable Cas9 to bind to DNA and inhibit transcription by blocking transcription initiation. This finding led to the development of specialized versions of Cas9 fused to repressor domains. Some companies have even developed versions fused to histone acetyltransferase (HAT) enabling shifts between heterochromatin and euchromatin states thus controlling gene activity.

When knocking down activity of key molecules, it can take a few days to be able to observe results. The endpoint of this experiment will involve analysis of cells for the activity of the molecule targeted. A sample data set with corresponding quiz will represent the post-laboratory work for this laboratory session.

NOTE: This experiment includes the use of actual, living cells. These cells must be worked with in the BIOSAFETY CABINET in the prep-room. Due to the ongoing pandemic, you will need to sterilize the space after each use. The added safety measures will be discussed as part of the lab introduction.

In this experiment you will prepare your work IN TRIPLICATE. This means you will need to calculate the proper volumes of your materials using the n + 2 rule. This rule refers to the idea that if you need a certain number of samples (n) you should prepare enough solution to cover two additional samples. For example, if you require enough materials to plate onto 3 wells (in triplicate), you will need to make enough mix for 5 samples. Use the blanks provided in the protocol to determine your final volumes. Remember, there will be 3 wells for a control without RNA as well as 3 wells for the Cas + RNA.

Key Materials and Terminology:
Synthetic guide RNA = RNA that determines your target; this laboratory will target
Transfection reagent = Solution that enables the material to get into the cell; this lab will utilize DharmaFECT reagent
Cas9 nuclease protein = This provides the activity necessary to inhibit transcription and thus knockdown the gene activity
Serum-free medium = Cells require specialized media for growth; experiments such as this often require additive-free media to function; Serum-free media enables the cells to remain healthy while being transfected

NOTEWORTHY INFORMATION: The discoveries and advances in CRISPR resulted in a Nobel Prize in Chemistry in 2020. It was awarded to both Dr. Jennifer Doudna and Dr. Emmanuelle Charpentier.

Pre-laboratory Questions:

1. Identify one primary research article that utilizes the CRISPR technology. In a single page report, summarize how the technology was used and what the findings were for the study. Provide a citation for the article as well as any additional sources that were used to create your summary.

PROCEDURE:

Begin the procedure by carefully labeling 5 microcentrifuge tubes in some way that enables you to differentiate between the mixes
- Cas + RNA working solution
- Cas – RNA working solution
- DharmaFECT Transfection Reagent
- Reaction Mix for CAS + RNA
- Reaction Mix for CAS – RNA

Prepare the Cas + RNA working solution

1. Add 2.5 ul of synthetic guide RNA per sample
   (_____ ul total)
2. Add 1 ul of Cas9 nuclease protein per sample
   (_____ ul total)
3. Add 46.5 ul of serum-free media per sample
   (_____ ul total)
4. Let the mixture sit on ice for 15 minutes while you prepare the control and DharmaFECT Transfection Reagent

Prepare the Cas – RNA working solution

1. Add 1 ul of Cas9 nuclease protein per sample
   (_____ ul total)
2. Add 49 ul of serum-free media per sample
   (_____ ul total)
3. Let the mixture sit on ice for 15 minutes while you prepare the DharmaFECT Transfection Reagent

Prepare the DharmaFECT Transfection Reagent

REMEMBER:
   You will need enough of this for BOTH the Cas + RNA AND Cas – RNA

1. Add 0.5 ul of DharmaFECT reagent per sample
   (_____ ul total)
2. Add 49.5 ul of serum-free media per sample
   (_____ ul total)
3. Let the mixture sit on ice until both previous reagents are ready

Generate the Reaction Mixtures for the 2 Treatment Conditions

Reaction Mix for CAS + RNA
 Add 50 ul per sample of the DharmaFECT reagent you prepared
  (_____ ul total)
 Add 50 ul per sample of the CAS + RNA you prepared
  (_____ ul total)

Reaction Mix for CAS – RNA
 Add 50 ul per sample of the DharmaFECT reagent you prepared
  (_____ ul total)
 Add 50 ul per sample of the CAS – RNA you prepared
  (_____ ul total)

Allow each mix to normalize to room temperature (incubate at room temperature for 10 minutes)

Once your mixes are prepared, you will need to plate them into the 96-well plate in the biosafety cabinet. Due to the ongoing pandemic, the biosafety cabinet will need to be sterilized with ethanol in between students. Please be patient and follow all instructions provided to you.

Add 100 ul of your mixes per well
 1. 3 wells for the CAS + RNA
 2. 3 wells for the CAS – RNA

Fill in the 96-well plate chart provided to indicate which wells contain your samples

Treatment requires a few days for it to decrease gene activity. Results will be provided to you as part of the post-lab assignment.

Post-Laboratory Exercise
Results from your experiment will be provided to you once available. You are expected to write a 1 page report with both a RESULTS and DISCUSSION section. Additional questions or expectations may be provided when the results are available.

Exercise 11
RNA Extraction

Objectives

1. Understand the Key Experimental Differences between Handling DNA and RNA
2. Improve your understanding of the role of RNA in cellular function

Introduction

Understanding how genes relate to disease is a multi-stage process that starts with the basics of the Central Dogma of Molecular Genetics: DNA is transcribed into RNA which is translated into protein. The presence or absence of a gene is the first component to the development of disease. Although different genes clearly have different consequences in development and disease, how does an organism produce a wide variety of cell types and function when every cell contains the same genetic information? The answer lies in the expression of genes.

Differential gene expression is what provides an organism with the enormous cellular diversity necessary for life in multi-cellular organisms. Gene expression is the production of RNA. The entire RNA complement of the cell is referred to as the Transcriptome. The first step to analyzing the Transcriptome or basic gene expression for specific genes is to extract the RNA from the cells.

Classic methods of RNA extraction involved utilizing Phenyl-Chloroform. This chemical has the potential to induce severe burns when spilled on the skin. As such, we will not be using this chemical. Instead, we will utilize an RNA extraction kit designed to yield high quantities of RNA from cells.

Unlike DNA, RNA is not very stable at room temperature; however, advances in the extraction procedures has enabled a transition for handling of RNA to room temperature rather than on ice in some cases. For this laboratory, you should plan to use ice to maintain the sample except where indicated in the protocol. It is imperative that you follow the instructions closely and note or indicate deviations from the procedure.

The RNA obtained using the method outlined in this exercise is particularly useful for complicated whole transcriptome analysis. All samples should be carefully handled and stored at -20°C until ready for future analysis. Contamination of samples with DNA or protein can significantly alter the ability to analyze the RNA or perform future procedures. As such, special preparations of our working space and materials will be performed.

Pre-Laboratory Questions

1. Explain why two different cell types from the same organism would have the same copies of a gene and yet have profoundly different concentrations of the corresponding RNA in the cell.

_____
_____
_____
_____
_____
_____
_____

2. Explain why two different cell types from the same organism would have the same DNA and yet have profoundly different RNA content.

_____
_____
_____
_____
_____
_____
_____

3. In the DNA extraction exercise, you learned about absorbance values and how they relate to DNA purity. Explain how these same values can be related to RNA and RNA purity. Be sure to explain how to determine RNA concentration via a mathematical formula.

_____
_____
_____
_____
_____
_____
_____
_____
_____

Procedure

1. Designate an area for working with RNA by outlining one part of the bench with tape

2. Prepare your station for working with RNA by carefully decontaminating it with 10% Bleach or UV light for 10 minutes (see specific instructions provided by your instructor)

3. Treat the area with an RNase decontaminating solution

4. Treat all materials including the pipetmen with an RNase decontaminating solution

5. Prepare your supplies by treating all pipetmen, tip boxes, and ice bucket with RNase decontaminating solution

6. Get a vial of MDA-MB-231 cells pelleted in 250 µl of lysis buffer containing β-mercaptoethanol from your instructor (RNA should be kept on ice so don't go to your instructor empty handed)

7. Homogenize your RNA sample via your hand-held, battery-operated mortar ON ICE (use short bursts to avoid splashing and loss of material)

8. Centrifuge the tubes at 12,000 x g for 2 minutes

9. Add 1 volume of 70% ethanol to the homogenate (250 µl)

10. Vortex to mix thoroughly and disperse any precipitate

11. Add the 500 µl of sample to a spin cartridge containing the membrane capable of selectively binding RNA

12. Centrifuge at 12,000 x g for approximately 15 seconds (just long enough to reach the desired speed for at least 2 seconds; use the quick spin option)

13. Discard the flow through, tap the collection tube relatively dry, and replace membrane cartridge into the collection tube

14. Add 700 µl Wash Buffer I to the column

15. Centrifuge at 12,000 x g (see step 12)

16. Discard the flow through, tap the collection tube relatively dry, and replace membrane cartridge into the collection tube

17. Add 500 µl of Wash Buffer II to the column

18. Centrifuge at 12,000 x g (see step 12)

19. Discard the flow through, tap the collection tube relatively dry, and replace membrane cartridge into the collection tube

20. Add 500 µl of Wash Buffer II to the column

21. Centrifuge at 12,000 x g (see step 12)

22. Discard the flow through, tap the collection tube relatively dry, and replace membrane cartridge into the collection tube

23. Centrifuge the empty tube at 12,000 x g for 2 minutes to dry the membrane bound with RNA

24. Discard the collection tube into the proper container and transfer the membrane to a new collection tube (the new tube is essential to obtaining pure RNA instead of a mixture contaminated with various buffers)

25. Add 50 µl of RNase-free water to the membrane and allow it to settle at room temperature for 1 minute

26. Centrifuge at 12,000 x g for 2 minutes to elute the RNA

27. Transfer the resulting flow through to a microcentrifuge tube labeled with 231 RNA, the date, and your initials (label both the top and side of your tube)

28. Transfer 2 µl into two cuvettes containing 198 µl water

29. Determine your RNA yield using spectrophotometry (read absorbance at 230 nm, 260 nm, and 280 nm)

Results

Record your absorbance values and RNA concentration and place the information into your notebook.

	Cuvette 1	Cuvette 2
RNA Concentration	_____	_____
Absorbance at 230 nm	_____	_____
Absorbance at 260 nm	_____	_____
Absorbance at 280 nm	_____	_____

Use the space below to record additional observations and results.

Post-Laboratory Assignment

Write a brief paragraph (less than 1 double-spaced page) explaining how your results relate to the quality of RNA you obtained. What conclusions can you draw from this brief exercise?

Depending on the availability of equipment, you may be proceeding with additional experiments on this RNA. Do you have high yield RNA or good quality? How can you tell if it is of "good" quality? Can you perform future experiments on your sample? Be sure to answer those questions in your paragraph.

Exercise 12
Basic Protein Extraction and Analysis

Objectives

1. Link DNA to Protein (Genotype to Phenotype)
2. Understand the Key Experimental Differences between Handling DNA and Protein

Introduction

Genes encode for information that makes functional products like proteins. In order to fully understand the impact of gene activity, it is important to understand the gene products. Genes exert their effects indirectly thus actual activity is carried out by the products of their activity, RNA and protein. Western analysis provides a relatively fast and accurate means of comparing protein content. Analyzing protein content enables scientists to answer a number of questions regarding gene activity and differences in gene expression.

Proteins can be isolated via a variety of extraction buffers. Given the relative instability of proteins it is important to extract them and maintain extracted proteins on ice. Since you have already isolated your protein, the next step is to make it possible to analyze the protein. Western analysis relies on gel electrophoresis to separate proteins by size. Proteins are run using SDS-PAGE (polyacrylamide gel electrophoresis). The proteins are separated by using an electric current exactly like the DNA electrophoresis described previously. Polyacrylamide differs from agarose in that polyacrylamide gels have smaller pore sizes and are generally stronger at separating smaller molecules.

The percentage of polyacrylamide in the gel determines the level of separation. Lower percentage gels separate larger proteins while higher percentage gels can separate significantly smaller proteins. Gradient gels can allow for optimal separation of all protein sizes in one gel.

In order to be able to verify proteins by size, a ladder with proteins of known size is also run in the gel. This control allows you to verify where in the gel each size protein is relative to the ladder. If the protein moved the same distance down the gel as the 70 kDa protein, you know your protein is approximately 70 kDa. By using a ladder that has multiple colors easily viewed in the gel, quick analysis of relative sizes is possible. In order to perform these comparisons, we need to be able to "see" the proteins. In order to visualize the proteins with our naked eyes, we can stain the gel using Coomassie Blue. This will give us a general idea of protein content including relative sizes. Further analysis of specific protein content can be performed via Western Analysis following transfer of the separated proteins to a membrane (see pre-laboratory questions and exercises 14 and 15).

Pre-Laboratory Questions

1. Explain why it is necessary to evaluate protein content even if you already know that the gene is there and transcription is taking place.

_____

_____

_____

_____

_____

_____

2. Gels come in a range of concentrations or percentages that enable different levels of separation of the material. If 8% is one of the lower percentages and 20% one of the higher, how well will a 10% gel separate small proteins versus larger proteins?

_____

_____

_____

_____

_____

Once proteins are separated, a means to further analyze the specific proteins present in the sample must be performed. In order to be able to analyze the proteins, they are transferred from the gel to a membrane. The membrane allows for us to probe the material for the presence of specific epitopes using antibodies. The most efficient means of transferring the proteins to a membrane is through the use of electric current in a process referred to as Western Analysis. In this procedure, the gel is sandwiched next to the membrane and a current is applied to force the proteins from the gel into the membrane. The membrane contains pores of very small size capable of trapping proteins within the gel.

3. Diagram a potential gel/membrane including a ladder. If you have a large protein, where in the gel would it end up? If you have a very small protein, where in the gel would it end up? Indicate large and small on your diagram.

4. As part of this experiment you are comparing reducing conditions to non-reducing conditions. Reducing conditions involve the addition of DTT or beta-mercaptoethanol to the loading dye. It has multiple functions including stabilizing the protein against higher temperatures and eliminating the net charge bias some proteins might exhibit.

   a. What might happen if your non-reducing sample contains proteins with a positive charge?

      _____
      _____
      _____
      _____
      _____
      _____

   b. What might happen if your non-reducing sample contains proteins with a negative charge?

      _____
      _____
      _____
      _____
      _____
      _____

   c. What might happen if your leave the proteins at room temperature for 3 days under reducing conditions verses non-reducing conditions?

      _____
      _____
      _____
      _____
      _____
      _____
      _____
      _____
      _____
      _____
      _____

Part A
Protein Extraction

Noteworthy Information

"I attribute my success to this: I never gave nor took any excuse."— Florence Nightingale

All of the steps of this full experiment (Parts A, B, and C) can be performed consecutively. This will take a great deal of time to complete so stay focused and follow any changes in the instructions made as the lab progresses. As always, if your procedure deviates in any way from the established procedure, indicate the change in your notebook.

Pre-laboratory Questions:
There are no pre-laboratory questions for this portion of the exercise (see previous section).

Procedure

1. Carefully label all of your tubes with the appropriate sample ID given to you

2. Prepare your RIPA Buffer by adding the appropriate amount of protease and phosphatase inhibitors (KEEP ON ICE)

3. Add 200 µl of the RIPA buffer to each tube careful to keep them on ice as much as possible

4. Follow your instructor to the prep room to sonicate your samples (hearing protection is required for this step so students will perform this in another area; be sure to indicate the specifics of your individual sonication in your procedure and notebook)

5. Spin samples at 1000 rpm for 2 minutes

6. Transfer your protein extract to your new, labeled tube

7. Aliquot 3 µl of the samples for analysis via the protein determination assay

Part B
Protein Determination Assay

Noteworthy Information

Although we will be able to get a relative idea of protein concentration in the gel through the Coomassie blue staining, this definitive quantification will enable us to use the protein in Western Analysis.

Procedure

8. Add 3 μl of sample to 27 μl of water

9. Add 10 μl of this mix and standards in triplicate to a 96-well plate as indicated in the diagram below

Standard 1	Water Only	Unknown 8	Unknown 16
Standard 2	Unknown 1	Unknown 9	Unknown 17
Standard 3	Unknown 2	Unknown 10	Unknown 18
Standard 4	Unknown 3	Unknown 11	Unknown 19
Standard 5	Unknown 4	Unknown 12	Unknown 20
Standard 6	Unknown 5	Unknown 13	Unknown 21
Standard 7	Unknown 6	Unknown 14	Unknown 22
Standard 8	Unknown 7	Unknown 15	Unknown 23

10. Mix parts component A to parts component B to generate the master mix

11. Add 200 μl of the master mix to each well containing standard and sample

12. Incubate the plate at 37°C for 30 minutes

13. Read the absorbance at 562 nm using a standard plate reader

14. Calculate your protein concentration using Excel as outlined by your instructor

Post-Laboratory Assignment

Using the information from the standards, generate a graph that represents the correlation between the concentration of the standard and the determined absorbance. Print the spreadsheet and graph you obtained from your analysis for your notebook. Use the graph and its corresponding information to generate a list of your samples and their corresponding concentrations to serve as a quick reference guide. This will be needed to run the gel and to perform further analysis. You will use this information in the generation of your final report (following completion of the final part of this total exercise).

Use the chart below for easy reference and summary:

Protein ID	Calculated Concentration	Actual Concentration (Dilution Factor Considered)	Volume of sample needed to have 25 ug of protein for a gel
Protein 1			
Protein 2			
Protein 3			
Protein 4			
Protein 5			
Protein 6			
Protein 7			
Protein 8			
Protein 9			
Protein 10			

Part C
Gel Electrophoresis

Noteworthy Information

This portion of the lab may be postponed until the Western Analysis Laboratory depending on the time constraints of the laboratory session. This is an excellent stopping point as calculations will need to be completed (from the previous section) in order to know the volume of sample should be added to each well. Protein samples can be frozen at -20°C until needed.

Pre-laboratory Questions:

There are no pre-laboratory questions for this portion of the exercise (see previous section).

Procedure

15. Mix 25 µg of protein per sample (based on the findings from the protein determination assay) with loading dye both with and without the reducing agent (β-mercaptoethanol) in a 1:3 ratio (1 part dye to 3 parts sample)

16. Rinse wells of gel set-up by your instructor

17. Load protein ladder (10 µl), controls (as indicated) and samples into wells of the SDS-PAGE gel (do NOT exceed 50 µl per well)

18. Run Gel at 100 volts for 45 minutes to 1 hour

19. Open the gel cartridge and transfer the gel to a weigh boat

20. Stain gel with 0.1% Coomassie Blue for 10 minutes

21. De-stain the gel with de-stain solution (50% methanol/10% Acetic Acid) until bands appear (may require overnight destaining)

22. Take a picture of your gel

Post-Laboratory Assignment

Complete a brief laboratory write-up regarding your findings. The write up should include the following sections: introduction, materials and methods, results, discussion, and future directions (see Appendix II).

Be sure to answer at least the following questions in your report:
1. What were your protein concentrations? Create a table to use as a figure in the report.
2. How do your results compare to other members of your group? We you more or less successful in extracting protein comparatively?
3. What does your gel tell you about your protein extraction?
4. Can you use the protein for future experiments? Why or why not?

All questions should be incorporated into the summary in paragraph form. This assignment is designed to incorporate scientific writing and assess your ability to summarize and explain results the way scientists do in scientific literature. Throughout the previous experiments, you have completed work that has been building toward this full reports. Be sure to look back at previous feedback and incorporate those ideas into your final product before submission. This report will be submitted either virtually or in person prior to the start of the next laboratory session.

Exercise 13
Classic Protein Purification

Objectives

Link DNA to Protein (Genotype to Phenotype)
Understand the Key Experimental Differences between Handling DNA and Protein
Learn a Method of Protein Isolation and Purification

Introduction

Although methods exist that allow analysis of the full protein content of cells, occasionally your needs require a single specific protein for further analysis or utilization. In order to analyze a single protein, it must be isolated and purified. Column Chromatography provides us a fast and easy method for isolating materials such as specific proteins.

In a previous lab, you may have generated green fluorescent protein (GFP) expressing bacteria. This laboratory exercise is designed to isolate that GFP for further use or analysis. The process is very similar to extraction techniques used in the past. The cells have to be opened to get the protein out, the protein must be protected from degradation, and all other cellular debris must be eliminated.

To accomplish these goals, this exercise is divided into protein extraction and protein isolation via column chromatography. The extraction procedure will break open the bacteria cells to isolate proteins. The column chromatography will purify the protein by exploiting hydrophobic interactions. The column in this procedure is the t-Butyl and Methyl Hydrophobic Interaction Chromatography Media column (HIC column).

The HIC column exploits conformational changes in the protein induced by changes in salt concentrations. High concentrations of salt allow for hydrophobic regions of GFP to be exposed and bind the media causing it to be retained in the column. Progressively lowering the salt concentration causes the protein to fold and "hide" the hydrophobic regions. This conformational change reduces the binding thus allowing the protein to be eluted from the column.

Pre-Laboratory Questions

1. Define the following terms
    a. Buffer -
    _____
    _____

    b. Purification -
    _____
    _____

    c. Chromatography -
    _____
    _____

    d. Hydrophobic Interaction -
    _____
    _____

2. Define Lysozyme and explain how it is utilized in this reaction. Be sure to include secondary components necessary to make the lysozyme function.
    _____
    _____
    _____
    _____
    _____
    _____
    _____
    _____
    _____
    _____
    _____

Part A
Protein Extraction

Noteworthy Information

"The most difficult thing is the decision to act, the rest is merely tenacity."— Amelia Earhart

Choosing both what you are going to do and how you are going to do it, is essential to successful science. You must use the right experiments to obtain your desired outcome. If, for example, you use a general extraction buffer in the exercise below, you may not be able to purify your protein using column chromatography.

Pre-laboratory Questions:

There are no pre-laboratory questions for this portion of the exercise (see previous section).

Procedure

1. Culture bacteria positive for GFP at 37°C on shaker at least overnight
2. Centrifuge the sample to pellet the bacteria
3. Discard supernatant and re-suspend pellet in TE buffer containing 0.5 mg/ml of lysozyme
4. Store at -20°C in aliquots of 750 µl
5. Thaw the bacteria and add 750 µl Binding Buffer (4M $(NH_4)_2SO_4$ in TE) per aliquot
6. Centrifuge at 14,000 rpm for 10 minutes
7. Isolate supernatant into fresh microcentrifuge tube

Part B
Column Purification

Noteworthy Information

"Life is 10% what happens to me and 90% of how I react to it."— Charles Swindoll

In this exercise, how the protein reacts to the solutions determines what will happen. Conformational changes, or changes in protein folding, enable us to exploit the basic properties of hydrophobicity.

.

Procedure

8. Equilibrate the column

    a. Drain the storage buffer

    b. Add 1.5 ml Equilibration Buffer (2M (NH4)2SO4 in TE)

    c. Allow the buffer to flow through

9. Load 500 µl of your cellular extract to the column

10. Collect the flow through into a labeled tube (Tube #1)

11. Wash the column with 500 µl Wash Buffer (1.3 M (NH4)2SO4 in TE)

12. Collect the flow through into a labeled tube (Tube #2)

13. Load 1 ml of elution buffer (TE Buffer) to the column

14. Collect the flow through into a labeled tube (Purified GFP)

15. Prepare your column for storage

    a. Load 1 ml of equilibration buffer

    b. Discard the flow through

    c. Cap the bottom of the column

    d. Load 500 µl of Equilibration Buffer

    e. Cap the top of the column

Post-Laboratory Assignment
There is no post-laboratory assignment for this section.

Exercise 14
Western Analysis

Objectives

1. Obtain an Understanding of the Applications of Gel Electrophoresis in Protein Analysis
2. Analyze Protein Content of Cells
3. Link Gene Expression with Protein Content

Introduction

Western Analysis involves "blotting" proteins onto a membrane for further analysis. Transferring proteins from a gel following gel electrophoresis enables not only long-term storage but also highly specific analysis of the protein content. There are two commercially available choices for membranes, nitrocellulose and polyvinylidene difluoride (PVDF). Once the proteins have been transferred to a membrane, highly specific detection of protein content can be performed by exploiting antibody-antigen interactions.

Key Terminology:
Antibodies = molecules produced by the immune system with high affinity towards a specific target
Primary antibody = first antibody in the procedure; directly binds the protein
Secondary antibody = binds the first/primary antibody by recognizing an epitope specific to the antibody rather than the sample
Antigen = a specific region or entire molecule that can be recognized by antibodies; a target for antibody reaction

The high specificity of the interaction between an antibody and its antigen allows us to identify proteins on the membrane. Antibody structure enables us to both target a specific antigen and visualize the binding. Antibodies have two regions of particular importance to this procedure: antibody binding sites (Fab region) and the constant region (the Fc region) that is distal from the Fab region. (These topics are explored in more detail in courses in basic immunology. Their importance to genetics lies in their genetic variability and their applications as a molecular tool.)

Although antibody-antigen interactions are highly specific, the membrane itself is not and non-specific binding of the antibody is possible. To prevent non-specific binding, membranes are "blocked" with a general buffer containing proteins capable of coating the membrane. Depending on the antibody, common choices including bovine serum albumin (BSA) or a powdered milk reconstituted in wash buffer.

Precautions must be taken in order to avoid accidental inhibition or deactivation of the antibodies. For example, BSA can completely block the activity and binding of secondary antibodies. To avoid these detrimental interactions, the membrane is "washed" in between steps. The wash buffer can be any one of the typical buffers for cell lines. A buffer becomes a "wash buffer" through the addition of a small amount of a mild detergent capable of gently removing unbound or excess materials. The two buffers utilized the most often are 1X PBS or 1X Tris-buffered Saline (TBS) containing 0.05% Tween 20 as the mild detergent.

Western analysis is incomplete unless we can visualize the presence or absence of antibody binding. Visualization or detection of antibody-antigen binding involves two main concepts.

1. DIRECT: A "detection" molecule can be directly conjugated to the Fc region of the primary antibody

2. INDIRECT: A secondary antibody targeted against the primary antibody is conjugated to a detection molecule

Specific detection of the binding can be through a variety of means regardless of whether it is a direct or indirect detection.

Colorimetric detection = linking the antibody to an enzyme that upon exposure to a reagent induces a chemical reaction that produces an insoluble pigment A common choice is, horse radish peroxidase (HRP). HRP when exposed to 4-chloronaphtol (Opti-4CN) undergoes an oxidation-reduction reaction to create an insoluble pigment that collects at the binding site of the target protein and allows visual identification.

Chemiluminescence detection = an enzyme-substrate reaction is used that emits light when exposed to a reagent; the light can be measured directly using a photoreceptor or indirectly by exposing autoradiography film and developing the film.

Fluorescence detection = the presences of a fluorophore that when stimulated with light at specific "excitation" wavelengths re-emits the light at a new wavelength. A variety of "colors" are available so it is theoretically possible to visualize more than one protein at a time.

This laboratory exercise can be adjusted to utilize any of the choices. It is written to be an indirect interaction involving chemiluminescence detection. A primary antibody against a protein will be selected. A highly specific secondary antibody conjugated to HRP will then be used. A chemilluminescence reagent combination will be added to the membrane briefly to trigger the chemical reaction and enable visualization of the binding reaction. This is one of the faster and cheaper methods of directly comparing protein content. It is highly reproducible and has been used in research for several years.

Unlike the previous lab where we were only interested in answering a yes or no, presence or absence or protein, question, western analysis seeks to determine differences in specific proteins and even in protein levels across samples. As such, certain controls must be present in every single gel that is transferred to a membrane for analysis. Every single membrane must have a protein ladder, a positive control, and a negative control. All negative controls should be protein samples that lack the protein of interest. All positive controls should be protein samples that contain the protein of interest. These controls enable the direct comparison of unknown samples and provide confirmation that what you are looking at is actually what you want to evaluate.

Pre-Laboratory Questions

1) Although antibody binding can be highly specific, there are two types of traditional antibodies, polyclonal and monoclonal. What is the difference between these two types of antibodies?

_____
_____
_____
_____
_____
_____

2) Diagram in the space provided or on an additional sheet what a membrane might look like if you have the following conditions (4 small diagrams are required to answer this question):
   a. 1 ladder and 3 general protein samples (a positive control, a negative control, and an unknown) analyzed with a polyclonal antibody
   b. 1 ladder and 3 general protein samples (a positive control, a negative control, and an unknown) analyzed with a monoclonal antibody
   c. 1 ladder and 3 purified protein samples (a positive control, a negative control, and an unknown) analyzed with a polyclonal antibody
   d. 1 ladder and 3 purified protein samples (a positive control, a negative control, and an unknown) analyzed with a monoclonal antibody

3) As part of an experiment, you are interested in determining whether your drug treated sample has a different level of protein expression from your untreated sample. Using the images below, what conclusions can you draw regarding your experiment? Be sure to indicate what data was used to make your conclusions (i.e. what information can NOT be removed from the figure below for you to be able to make direct comparisons?).

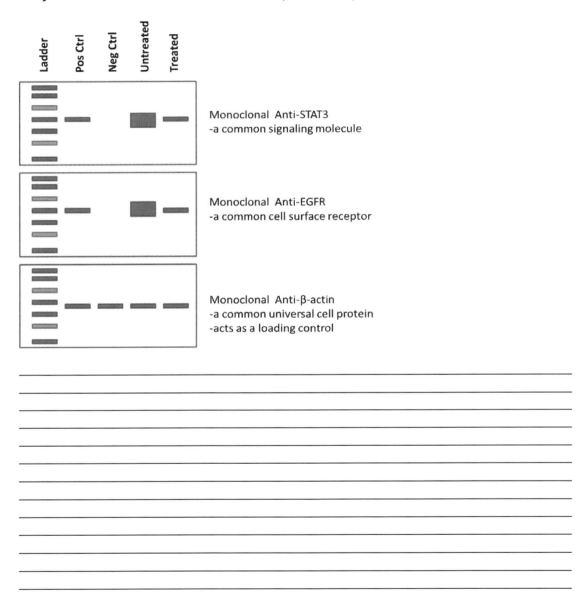

Monoclonal Anti-STAT3
-a common signaling molecule

Monoclonal Anti-EGFR
-a common cell surface receptor

Monoclonal Anti-β-actin
-a common universal cell protein
-acts as a loading control

_____
_____
_____
_____
_____
_____
_____
_____
_____
_____
_____
_____
_____
_____

Part A
Protein Separation

Pre-laboratory Questions:

There are no pre-laboratory questions for this portion of the exercise (see previous section).

Procedure

1. Determine the volume of sample necessary to obtain 25 µg of protein extract for each of your samples

2. Mix 3 parts sample to 1 part loading dye

3. Heat on heat block warmed to 95°C for 5 minutes

4. Place gel into electrophoresis unit, fill unit with 1X Running Buffer, and carefully rinse wells with buffer using a p200 gel-loading microtip

5. Load protein ladder, controls, and samples into wells (be sure to create a diagram to keep track of what you load into each well)

6. Run the gel at 100 volts for 45 minutes to 1 hour

Part B
Protein Transfer

Noteworthy Information

It is critical that all air bubbles be removed throughout this procedure. Keeping the entire "sandwich" submerged in a small amount of transfer buffer, is a great way to ensure proper elimination of air bubbles. Each layer of the "sandwich" should be pressed to eliminate bubbles and ensure equal distribution of charge across the entire gel and membrane.

Pre-laboratory Questions:

There are no pre-laboratory questions for this portion of the exercise (see previous section).

Procedure

7. During the run prepare the "sandwich" required for the transfer

    a. Wet 6 squares of filter paper, two sponges, and the membrane in 1X Transfer Buffer for at least 15 minutes (if using a PVDF membrane be sure to activate the membrane with 100% methanol for 30 seconds before equilibrating it in 1X Transfer Buffer)

    b. Place one sponge and 3 sheets of filter paper on the black side of the apparatus

    c. Leave the other 3 sheets of filter paper and membrane to the side until gel is finished running

8. Carefully snap open the gel apparatus and transfer the gel to the top of the filter paper you set-up in 1X Transfer Buffer (be sure to have the ladder to the right of the "sandwich" to get it to transfer to the left of the membrane; well 1 on far right of the "sandwich" so it sits on far left in the membrane)

9. Place the membrane on top of the gel and cover with the remaining filter paper

10. Place the second sponge on the filter paper and remove air bubble by carefully rolling a tube over the "sandwich"

11. Close the apparatus (Membrane should be closest to the clear side and the gel should be closest to the black side)

12. Load the sandwich to the Transfer apparatus with a small amount of 1X Transfer Buffer in the bottom (match black to black and clear to red)

13. Add the ice pack and finish filling the rig with 1X Transfer Buffer

14. Run the transfer at 100V and 4°C for 1 hour (Alternative options: 10V overnight; 80 V for 2 hours; 30V for 3 hours)

Part A
Protein Detection

Pre-laboratory Questions:

There are no pre-laboratory questions for this portion of the exercise (see previous section).

Procedure

15. Carefully open the "sandwich" and peel your membrane away from your gel

16. Cut excess portions of the membrane and transfer the membrane to a shallow container

17. Block the membrane in 5% Milk in 0.05% TBSt overnight at 4°C on a shaker if possible (if extended incubation is required, do not allow the milk to evaporate or settle as it can coat the membrane too thickly)

18. Discard blocking solution and rinse quickly in 0.05% TBSt

19. Add primary antibody (1:1000) in 5% milk in 0.05% TBSt or 5% BSA in 0.05% TBSt to the membrane

20. Incubate on orbital shaker for 1 hour at room temperature

21. Wash the membrane in 0.05% TBSt: 1 time quick and 3 times for 5 minute each shaking on an orbital shaker each time (discard wash solution in between each wash)

22. Add secondary antibody (1:5000) to the membrane in 5% milk in 0.05% TBSt

23. Incubate on orbital shaker for 30 minutes to 1 hour at room temperature

24. Wash the membrane in 0.05% TBSt: 1 time quick and 3 times for 5 minute each shaking on an orbital shaker each time (discard wash solution in between each wash)

25. Mix 1 part solution A to 1 part solution B to generate the developer; add 1 ml of the mixture to the membrane for 1 minute

26. Place the membrane into the film cassette and travel to the darkroom for developing

27. Expose film to the membrane for 1, 2, 5, and 10 minutes (to conserve film multiple membranes will be placed in the same cassette; students will travel in small groups to complete this portion of the exercise)

28. Trace your protein ladder onto your film and label your lanes

29. Scan your films and obtain an electronic copy of the images

Post-Laboratory Assignment

Complete a brief laboratory write-up regarding your findings. The write up should include the following sections: introduction, materials and methods, results, discussion, and future directions.

Be sure to answer at least the following questions in your report:
1. What is the approximate size of your protein? Is the size what you expect based on what you know about your protein of interest?
2. How do your samples compare to the positive and negative controls?
3. How do the individual samples compare to one another within the membrane?
4. What conclusions can you draw with the information obtained thus far in the analysis?

Exercise 15
Western Analysis Re-Blot

Objectives

1. Learn comparative analysis techniques for Western Analysis
2. Compare protein content and link this to cellular function

Introduction

In order to truly analyze and compare differences in protein content, a control protein known to be present in all samples must be analyzed to use in the comparison. This control protein serves as both a loading control and as a means to verify the presence of protein in general. Remember, all negative controls should be protein samples that lack the protein of interest and all positive controls should be protein samples that contain the protein of interest. Although a "blank" well makes a good control for loaded and unloaded gels, it is not a true negative control.

In theory, a membrane can be re-blotted an indefinite number of times. In reality, each time you "strip" the membrane, you remove some of the protein and reduce the ability of antibodies to bind. Due to this, we always start the analysis with the antibody believed to bind the weakest and move toward the antibody that binds the strongest. If you started with a common protein such as β-actin, you will not be able to adequately eliminate the previous binding to see the second antibody-antigen reaction. Generally, a membrane can be stained 3 times without significant loss of binding affinity.

This exercise continues the previous exercise and seeks to explore changes in protein content across a series of treated and untreated samples. It is possible to perform additional analyses using these steps. The procedure can be repeated as many times as is desired; however, it is written as the final step with β-actin as the control protein.

Pre-Laboratory Questions

What you have been waiting for all semester; there are no pre-laboratory questions for this exercise at all. You already have a good idea of what to expect so simply complete your previous lab assignment.

Procedure

1. Strip your membrane of the previous antibodies by adding 10 ml of stripping buffer to the membrane in a western container

2. Incubate on a shaker for 5 to 10 minutes (for weakly bound proteins less time is required)

3. Re-block the membrane by incubating the membrane in 5 ml 5% milk in 0.05% TBSt for 1 hour

4. Discard blocking solution and rinse quickly in 0.05% TBSt

5. Add primary antibody (1:1000) in 5% milk in 0.05% TBSt to the membrane

6. Incubate on orbital shaker for 1 hour at room temperature

7. Wash the membrane in 0.05% TBSt: 1 time quick and 3 times for 5 minute each shaking on an orbital shaker each time (discard wash solution in between each wash)

8. Add secondary antibody (1:5000) to the membrane in 5% milk in 0.05% TBSt

9. Incubate on orbital shaker for 30 minutes to 1 hour at room temperature

10. Wash the membrane in 0.05% TBSt: 1 time quick and 3 times for 5 minute each shaking on an orbital shaker each time (discard wash solution in between each wash)

11. Mix 1 part solution A to 1 part solution B to generate the developer; add 1 ml of the mixture to the membrane for 1 minute

12. Place the membrane into the film cassette and travel to the darkroom for developing

13. Expose film to the membrane for 1, 2, 5, and 10 minutes (to conserve film, multiple membranes will be placed in the same cassette; students will travel in small groups to complete this portion of the exercise)

14. Trace your protein ladder onto your film and label your lanes

15. Scan your films and obtain an electronic copy of the images

Use the space below to record any observations or changes to the protocol.

Post-Laboratory Assignment

Revise the brief laboratory write-up from the previous exercise. The write up should still include the following sections: introduction, materials and methods, results, discussion, and future directions with edits that include the information from this lab and figures from both exercises.

Be sure to answer at least the following questions in your report:
1. What is the approximate size of your protein(s)? Is the size what you expect based on what you know about your protein(s) of interest?
2. How do your samples compare to the positive and negative controls?
3. How do the individual samples compare to one another within the membrane?
4. What conclusions can you draw?

Additional Analysis (optional extra credit)

Analyze your scanned pictures using analysis software. Using software such as Image J, you can obtain quantifiable results of band density. Tutorials on how to perform this analysis will be provided during the incubation periods of the lab exercise. This is a cheaper version of dense cytometry. Use the quantified results to compare the ratio of protein concentration to the loading control. Incorporate these results into your lab report via appropriate graphs.

Appendix I:
Lab Equipment Overview

Microcentrifuge tubes
Variety of sizes: 0.5 ml, 1.5 ml, and 2 ml

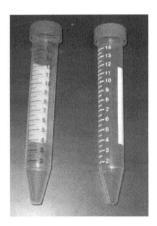

15 ml centrifuge tubes
Variety of options
Maximum volume = 15 ml

50 ml centrifuge tubes
Variety of options
Maximum volume = 50 ml

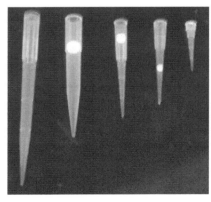

Microtips
Barrier and non-barrier options
Sizes: 1000 µl, 200 µl, 20 µl, and 10 µl

Basic Vortex
Can operate continuously or by touch
Variety of speeds for gentle verses severe vortexing

Orbital Shaker
Variety of speeds for gentle verses severe shaking/mixing
There are a variety of options available with different appearances

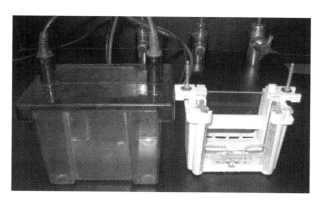

Western Analysis Rig
Gel Electrophoresis Unit
Variety of options available

Plate Reader
5 filter capacity
Can read absorbance at wavelengths equal to the included filters

 **96 well plate**

 **Electronic Mortar and Pestal**
Useful in grinding tissues and processing
materials for extraction

 **Waste Bucket**

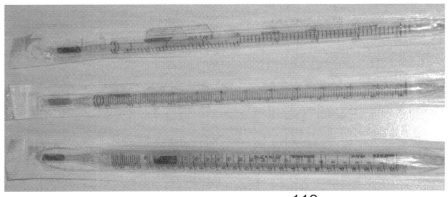 **Pipets**
From Top to
Bottom:
5 ml
10 ml
25 ml

Emergency Eye Wash:

Requires assistance to use it

Biosafety Cabinet

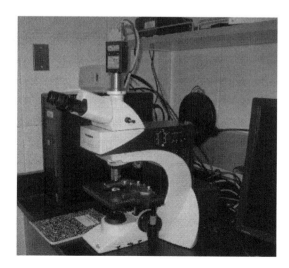

Microscope and Fluorescent Light

Computer includes Cytovision for analysis of chromosome spreads

113

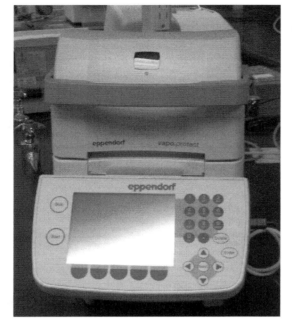

Thermocycler for PCR

Appendix II:
Contents of a Basic Lab Report

Introduction

Use this section to give the reader the "big picture" as well as any background we may need to understand the experimental question. These can be brief but should include properly cited references.

Materials and Methods

A scaled-down version of what you actually did in the exercise. It is not a copy of the procedure but a summary of key steps in paragraph form.

Results

Your actual findings summarized with figures when appropriate. All figures must have titles and figure legends explaining the figure.

Discussion

This section is all about putting your results into a broader context. What conclusions were you able to draw? How do your conclusions relate to the "big picture" you outlined in your introduction?

Future Directions

This is about defining the next step for yourself and the research. Where should the research go next? What should you do next? If the experiment did not work, what is the most obvious next step for you hypothetically?

Appendix III:
References

1. M. H. Oliver, N. K. Harrison, J. E. Bishop, P. J. Cole, G. J. Laurent, A rapid and convenient assay for counting cells cultured in microwell plates: application for assessment of growth factors. *J Cell Sci* **92 (Pt 3)**, 513-518 (1989).
2. T. S. Becker, S. Rinkwitz, Zebrafish as a genomics model for human neurological and polygenic disorders. *Dev Neurobiol* **72**, 415-428 (2012).
3. S. Younes, A. Al-Sulaiti, E. A. A. Nasser, H. Najjar, L. Kamareddine, Drosophila as a Model Organism in Host-Pathogen Interaction Studies. *Front Cell Infect Microbiol* **10**, 214 (2020).
4. S. E. Bates, Classical cytogenetics: karyotyping techniques. *Methods Mol Biol* **767**, 177-190 (2011).
5. V. L. Lazarevic, B. Johansson, Why classical cytogenetics still matters in acute myeloid leukemia. *Expert Rev Hematol* **13**, 95-97 (2020).
6. L. Zhang *et al.*, Chromosomal changes detected by fluorescence in situ hybridization in patients with acute lymphoblastic leukemia. *Chin Med J (Engl)* **116**, 1298-1303 (2003).
7. A. J. Bronkhorst, V. Ungerer, S. Holdenrieder, Comparison of methods for the quantification of cell-free DNA isolated from cell culture supernatant. *Tumour Biol* **41**, 1010428319866369 (2019).
8. D. Kumar, M. K. Panigrahi, M. Suryavanshi, A. Mehta, K. K. Saikia, Quantification of DNA Extracted from Formalin Fixed Paraffin-Embeded Tissue Comparison of Three Techniques: Effect on PCR Efficiency. *J Clin Diagn Res* **10**, BC01-BC03 (2016).
9. C. Perez-Barrios *et al.*, Comparison of methods for circulating cell-free DNA isolation using blood from cancer patients: impact on biomarker testing. *Transl Lung Cancer Res* **5**, 665-672 (2016).
10. W. W. Wilfinger, K. Mackey, P. Chomczynski, Effect of pH and ionic strength on the spectrophotometric assessment of nucleic acid purity. *Biotechniques* **22**, 474-476, 478-481 (1997).
11. B. Wiedenheft *et al.*, Structural basis for DNase activity of a conserved protein implicated in CRISPR-mediated genome defense. *Structure* **17**, 904-912 (2009).

Made in the USA
Monee, IL
03 July 2021